Once upon a dark and stormy night....

Writing Fiction

Anita Burns

I dedicate this book to the brave souls in my writer's critique group. Heartfelt thanks to Judy Mcallister, Carol J. Amato, David Lintner, Amanda Baker, Michele Iqbal, Amy Waterman, Kristin Roybal, and Kitty Ayers.

Without you, and your infinite patience, eagle eyes, and amazing skills, I would still be wishing I could be a writer.

Extended Table of Contents

.9.Characters..63

A Note from the Author

Even though this book has been edited, read, and spell-checked multiple times and by at least eight people, it is inevitable that we missed *something*.

If you discover an error, just smile and enjoy your Sherlock-like sharp-eyed skills, and drop me a note at anitaburns1@gmail.com to let me know what you found so I can correct it.

Once Upon a Dark and Stormy Night

Writing Fiction

Introduction

I originally meant to create a simple and brief guide for my Dark and Stormy Night writing workshops but as I wrote, it grew into something more—a concise, to-the-point, and easily understandable resource for any writer of fiction—especially indie authors.

When I first dipped my toe into the deep end of the fiction-book pool, I sank to the bottom like a stone. My writing had promise but any talent I had was hidden beneath a mound of ignorance about the techniques of crafting fiction.

What makes it tough for some writers, though, is the delusional Dunning-Kruger effect that has some budding authors thinking they're more talented than they are. This astounding phenomenon creates high-ratings for entertainment TV talent shows who are fascinated by the odd confidence so many talentless people display.Young hopeful singers may sound like caterwauling to us, but the screeching contestants believe they possess the chops to be the next Elvis or Katy Perry.

Your willingness to accept critique from others and learning how great authors do what they do can open your eyes and train your mind to be more objective about your work.

The best way to hone your craft is to join a good critique

group. Find one with members who can give and receive constructive criticism.

The critique groups I belong to have been invaluable. Like metal smiths, we hammer away at rough materials to create something beautiful.

With determination, I set out on a path of hard work, study, practice, and pounding the keys. I offered my prose up for critique and editorial suggestions then rewrote until my fingers grew numb. I learned to navigate the tapestry of complex patterns that help authors weave compelling and engrossing stories.

Unfortunately, not all critique groups manage themselves professionally. I've been in a few where the participants are more interested in socializing than offering and receiving constructive feedback. Socializing might fulfill your friendship needs, but it's usually a waste of time for improving your skills.

Whether you hone and polish your writing by attending a critique group, hire an editor, or wing it on your own, continue learning your craft and keep writing. Hopefully, all the ingredients will come together. At the same time, be wary of the perfection trap. No book is free from flaw. Even best-sellers and world-famous novels have errors or issues that would make your English teacher cluck her tongue. Readers are forgiving of minor infractions, such as the occasional alliteration, typo, or incomplete sentence. Do your best but don't fret for years over every comma.

Quick Tips

Below is a random list of tips as quick reminders. You'll find more on each one in the following chapters.

- Make each chapter, scene, and paragraph relevant to the story, have something at stake, and/or give insight into a character.

- Every word must count. Eliminate any that don't add to the flow, are repetitive, or unnecessary.

- As much as possible, show instead of tell.

- There must be conflict. Ask yourself, "What's at stake?" Conflict can be external or internal, strong or mild.

- Put the reader inside the point of-view (POV) character's head.

- For novels with multiple POV, use only one per scene. Romance novels are an exception to this. And some authors are masters of multiple POV writing, Nora Roberts is an example. It's not easy to do well.

- Give each character's dialogue or action its own paragraph.

- Use quotation marks for external dialogue and italics for internal dialogue.

- Tighten up. Eliminate unneeded words,

descriptions and dialogue.

- Generally, keep back story brief or bring it out gradually throughout the book.

- Minimize repeating words and phrases.

- Proof your draft at least twice—once for grammar, spelling, and punctuation, then again for content and continuity. Stephen King wrote that he sometimes proofs his work and rewrites ten times.

- If you are going to self-publish, find someone knowledgeable to proof and edit your manuscript.

- If you self-publish, have a professional format the book and design the cover. If you use any unorthodox formatting, be consistent.

Genre

Before you put pen to paper or fingers to keys, a good practice is to decide what category (genre) your story fits into—or not.

Publishers and sellers use genres and sub-categories to decide how to market and where shelve your book.

If you self-publish, this is less of an issue. Although *Amazon.com* and other distributors will put your work up for sale no matter what, choosing a genre and adding multiple tags (descriptive keywords) are help readers find your book more easily.

So, what are the genres? It depends on whose list you read. There are hundreds listed by various publishers and websites. In modern writing, pure genres are less common than they were prior to the late 20th century. Many authors combine them in the same book, i.e. Western/Mystery, Vampire/Romance, Science Fiction/Thriller.

What genre or genres does your story fit into? You might find it a combination of more than one (cross genre). This is common in modern writing. An example is Stephen King's, *11/22/63*, a time travel book about the Kennedy assassination, it crosses Mystery, Thriller, Suspense, and Historical genres.

Below is a partial list of the most common genres.

Adventure—Bold, dashing, daring, and often set in exotic locations. A hero or heroine saves the day after facing danger and seemingly impossible odds.

Examples

The Miracle Man, Todd Easterling

Classic: *Moby Dick,* Herman Melville

Children's Fiction—Written for children of specific ages, from a child's point of view (POV), and/or featuring children as main characters. Subgenres include Young Adult (YA), Tween, and New Adult. Books for very small children are mostly images with little writing.

Examples

Small Children: *Nonni's Moon,* Julia Inserro and Lucy Smith

Older children: *The Phantom Hunters: #1 The Lost Treasure of the Golden Sun,* Carol J. Amato

Classic: *The House at Pooh Corner,* A.A. Milne

Crime/Detective—showcase a crime, how the criminal gets caught, and the repercussions of the crime.

Examples

Frankie, Molly Dillon

Classic: *The Big Sleep,* Raymond Chandler

Fantasy—Strange or otherworldly settings or characters.

Examples

A Spell for Chameleon, Piers Anthony

Classic: *Alice's Adventures in Wonderland,* Lewis Carroll

Historical—Historical settings. Often based on actual events, they can include fictional or fictionalized characters.

Examples

When Dreams Take Flight, Judith McAllister

Classic: *The Good Earth,* Pearl S. Buck

Horror—Dread, fear, shock. Fast-paced writing

Examples

Finders Keepers, Stephen King

Classic: *Frankenstein,* Mary Shelley

Humor—Meant to entertain and evoke laughter through subtle, slapstick, absurd, or ironic humor.

Examples

The Hitchhiker's Guide to the Galaxy, Douglas Adams

Classic: *My Man Jeeves,* P.G. Wodehouse

Mystery/Crime—The protagonist solves a crime, reveals secrets, or unravels a mystery.

Examples

The Da Vinci Code: A Novel, Robert Langdon

Classic: *The Maltese Falcon,* Dashiell Hammett

Religious/Spiritual—Religious or spiritual with morality lessons interwoven with another genre.

Examples

Real Trust—A Clean Inspirational Christian Romance, Erich Jade

Classic: *The Screwtape Letters,* C.S. Lewis

Romance—Typically, two main characters fall in love and live "happily ever after." Stories are often variations of "boy-meets-girl, boy-loses-girl, boy-wins-girl-back." Romance novels almost always have a happy ending.

Stubborn Love, Wendy Owens
Classic: *Jane Eyre,* Charlotte Bronte.

Science Fiction (Sci Fi)—Real or imagined science, usually futuristic, and set all or partially on other planets.
Examples
Foundation, Isaac Asimov
Classic: *The Time Machine,* H.G. Wells

Sci Fi Dystopian—Set against a backdrop of a worldwide disaster where civilization we know has been destroyed. The characters play out the story in a post-apocalyptic world.
Examples:
The Last Survivors: A Dystopian Society in a Post Apocalyptic World, Bobby Adair
Classic: *Farenheit 451,* Ray Bradbury

Short story—Often only a few scenes long, dealing with a small cast of characters. Mood is more important than plot. Sometimes short stories are published in collections of the author's work.
Examples
Glitch, Hugh Howey
Classic: *The Chrysalis,* Ray Bradbury

Suspense/Thriller—The protagonist is in danger, although he/she might not know it at first. This genre is related to Mystery and integrated in the same book.

Examples

Ashley Bell: A Novel, Dean Koontz

Classic: *The Hunt for Red October,* Tom Clancy

Western—Nearly always set in the American Old West in the late eighteenth to early twentieth century.

Examples

The Whip: Inspired by the Story of Charley Parkhurst, Karen Kondazian

Classic: *Last of the Breed,* Louis L'amour

Research online for genres to find more.

Cross-Genres

In the ever changing world of publishing, some classifications have developed fuzzy edges. For example, it's difficult to separate suspense, thriller, and mystery. Most of them seem to have elements of all three. Modern authors—and some classic novelists—mix genres together to form interesting combinations, such as Mystery/Western, Romance/Thriller, Crime/Historical, and more. For example, Amanda Ashley writes award-winning, Vampire/Paranormal/Romance books.

Genres aside, hundreds of thousands of books have been written using the same general plot. Classification is just a way for publishers, booksellers, and readers to know a book's overarching style, form, and content. So, even though a romance can be set in the American Old West, or a thriller can be set in space, a general idea of what category your book fits into helps sellers, publishers, and readers.

A Deeper look at the Top-Selling Genres

#1 Romance

Typically 40,000 to 100,000 words.

Plot generally focuses on two main characters.

Usually told from hero's and the heroine's points of view. Sometimes the characters fall in love first then face conflict before getting together. Sometimes the conflict comes first then love blossoms.

Typical Romance Plot

- Hero and heroine dislike each other at first but there is a strong attraction, anyway.
- They are forced together by some circumstance.
- They begin to fall in love or at least acknowledge their attraction to each other.
- There is an obstacle that keeps them apart.
- Obstacles and challenges are met and overcome. The hero and heroine come together and live happily ever after.

#2 Crime/Mystery/Suspense

Typically 70,000 to 90,000 words.

The reader takes part in solving the crime or mystery.

- Generally, no romance, but there may be flirtations or sex.
- The antagonist (criminal, murderer, world-destroyer, mad scientist, etc.) must be discovered by logical deduction and rational science rather than through accident, the paranormal (except in the Paranormal/

Mystery genre), or coincidence. The Perry Mason model of the guilty man/woman jumping up in court and unexpectedly confessing is outdated. It makes the reader feel cheated.

- Misdirection and red herrings are included to throw the detective and the reader off the scent.
- There must be a mystery solver, detective, or investigator—usually the main character—who helps the reader discover and navigate through clues that lead to solving the mystery.
- There has to be at least one corpse, missing person, mystery, or a puzzle to solve.
- The culprit cannot be a surprise character that played no part in the rest of the book.
- The writing should be clean, direct, and to the point. No meandering into side stories.
- Whether you show the crime so the reader already knows who did it and it becomes a game of cat and mouse or withhold "who done it" until it is discovered is a matter of choice. Crime/Mystery/Suspense is a game where the reader becomes a player.

#3 Religion/Spiritual

Word count can vary from 50,000 to 140,000 words.

- These stories take place in a religious/spiritual setting that follows the same guidelines for whatever other genre the book fits into.
- They can be mysteries, romances, literary, science fiction, or just about anything else.
- The religious/spiritual subject is inserted into the material as an over-arching theme.

#4 Science Fiction/Fantasy

- Science Fiction and Fantasy are related but have definite differences.
- Science fiction is about technology, future, and/or science.
- It can be as imaginary as the author wants but must have some logic and a strong possibility factor that relates to scientific theory.
- Often, Science Fiction is set in a post-apocalyptic world.

Fantasy is probably the oldest fiction genre, dating back to ancient times.

- It can be found in fairy tales and mythological sagas. Some of these are so old they're considered by many as historical rather than mythological. *The Mahabarata*, an ancient Indian saga, is an example.
- Fantasy can be as bizarre as the author wants it to be. It has no obligation to adhere to any logic or scientific theory. An excellent example are the *Xanth* novels by Piers Anthony. Also, J. K. Rowling's Harry Potter series fits this category.
- Fantasy novels often contain, wizards, witches, paranormal beings, fairies, angels, superheroes, dragons, inter-dimensional beings, and such.
- Crossovers between science fiction and fantasy are also popular. A good example is Frank Herbert's *Dune* series.
- Plot lines for these genres follow the same as novels in general: A problem, a hero or heroine, overcoming obstacles, resolution, and ending.

#5 Horror/Thriller

Word count from 80,000 to 100,000 words.

- Horror/thriller plots follow the same rules as novels but they are written to create suspense, and instill fear and shock in the reader. The creepier, more shocking, more surprising, the better.
- Sentences are short and concise.
- Tension drives the horror novel. There is never a rest, never a time of peace that isn't suddenly interrupted by something shocking and dangerous.

A Look at Literary Fiction

According to *Huffington Post* writer, Steven Petite, there are two kinds of fiction: Genre and Literary.

Literary is notoriously difficult to classify. To many, it is a category for anything that doesn't fit into a genre or sub-genre.

If you search the Internet, it becomes evident that Literary Fiction includes the most award-winning and critically acclaimed books of all time.

There are many opinions about what constitutes Literary Fiction versus Genre Fiction. Most bloggers and publishing professionals who write on the topic seem to agree that Literary is character-driven and Genre is more plot-driven. However you interpret this, there are some definite ideas about what constitutes a Literary book.

Literary Fiction

- Literary word count can be 80,000 to over 100,000 words—Leo Tolstoy's *War and Peace* is a whopping 587,287 words.

- Stories can be told in a wide variety of ways. They can be insightful, thoughtful, philosophical.
- Subplots, side stories, and meaningful meanderings are acceptable.

Literary fiction is character-driven.

- Typically, action is slower and more attention is given to the character's emotions, inner workings, and motivations. The inner story is foremost.
- Plots can be complex and often focus on social issues.
- Writing can have an almost poetic or lyrical quality.
- Although it can contain humor, literary fiction is usually serious and often dark.

A Few Examples of Literary Fiction

The Great Gatsby, F. Scott Fitzgerald, 47,094 words

To Kill a Mockingbird, Harper Lee, 100,388 words

The Kite Runner, Khaled Hosseini, 106,895 words

Slaughterhouse Five, Kurt Vonnegut, 49,459 words

Of Mice and Men, John Steinbeck, 30,000 words

The Book Thief, Markus Zusak, 144,000 words

Memoirs of a Geisha, Arthur Golden, 186,418 words

The Old Man and the Sea, Ernest Hemingway, 26,720 words (more short story than book)

Lolita, Vladimir Nabokov, 112,473 words

The list of memorable and "important" literature in this genre could go on into the hundreds.

.2.

Point of View

There are many ways to write your book. One of the first things to consider is Point of View (POV). In other words, who will be telling the story? Whose head(s) will you be in?

A book can be written entirely from one POV or from many. A good sources is *Writer's Digest.com*.

Although there are many variations, and just as many opinions about the right or wrong way to handle POV, typically, authors write from one of the three main categories:

First person

In this style, one character tells the whole story from his/her POV. It uses pronouns, "I", "me," "my," and "mine."

First Person

> My uncle's farm had been neglected since Aunt Sybel died in the fall of '09, so I put city life behind me and drove out to the Kansas homestead where I was born.
>
> The wide, dirt driveway looked the same and the rambling farmhouse hadn't changed much, except for

needing a new coat of paint. Chickens still roamed free, clucking and scratching in the dirt for a tasty snack.

I stepped out of the car, shaded my eyes with a hand, and gazed at the fields. The acres of sunflowers, nearly choked with weeds, seemed to cry out for help.

As I turned my attention back to the house, I spied John, the old caretaker, eyeing me from behind the rusty screen door. My heart dropped. *I hope he doesn't think I'm going to put him out to pasture. I'll need his help to get this place back in shape.*

Books Written in First Person

- *The Hunger Games,* Suzanne Collins
- *To Kill a Mockingbird,* Harper Lee
- *Twilight,* Stephenie Meyer
- *Outlander,* Diana Gabaldon

Second Person

This is an unpopular format for fiction. It uses the pronouns, "you," "your," and "yours." Second Person POV is someone telling the story as if he/she were speaking directly to another person about their experience.

Second Person

Your uncle's farm had been neglected since your Aunt Sybel died in the fall of '09, so you put city life behind and drove out to the Kansas homestead where you were born. You noticed that the wide, dirt driveway looked the same and the rambling farmhouse hadn't changed much, except for needing a new coat of paint. Chickens still roamed free, clucking and scratching in the dirt for a tasty snack.

You stepped out of the car, shaded your eyes with a

hand and gazed at the fields. The acres of sunflowers, nearly choked with weeds, seemed to cry out for help.

As you turned your attention back to the house, you spied John, the old caretaker, eyeing you from behind the rusty screen door. Your heart dropped and you thought, *I hope he doesn't think I'm going to put him out to pasture. I'll need his help to get this place back in shape.*

Books Written in Second Person
- *Bright Lights Big City,* Jay McInerney
- *The Diver's Clothes Lie Empty,* Vandela Vida
- *Layla,* Nina de la Mer

Third Person

Third Person is the most popular POV and the most complex. Here, an unseen observer, usually the author, narrates the story from the thoughts and feelings of one or more characters.

This style uses the pronouns, "he," "she," "him," "they," "them," "his," her(s)," "us," and "its." In Third Person, there is a fine line between telling the story from a character's eyes and the author intruding. (See chapter 14 Author Intrusion).

Third Person POV is generally split into four categories: Multiple, Omniscient, Limited, and Observational, but the most popular are Multiple and Limited. These two styles are so close they are often confused with each other. If you venture into research on these two styles, you will find tutorials, books, and blogs describing Omniscient when it is actually Multiple and vice versa. The difference is small but important.

Third Person Multiple, and Omniscient

In both styles, the narrator is allowed inside more than one character's heads.

Each change of POV is usually established at the beginning of a new scene or chapter, although when a switch from one head to another happens within a scene, there should be a cue, marked with a scene-break symbol (asterisk, hash-tag mark, or an extra space between paragraphs). This prevents reader confusion.

What Not To Do

Sam inspected the grass on the course. "I haven't seen this kind before." He gazed across the green. *I hope they didn't go for Poa Annua. It'll need more water than we can spare in this drought.* "I wonder how this will hold up during the tournament?" Joe crouched down and ran his hand over the stiff blades.

In the above, it's unclear if Sam is saying "I wonder…." Or if it is Joe.

Reading further could clear it. But having to figure out what an author means is not what readers want.

Reworked

> Sam inspected the grass on the course. "I haven't seen this kind before." He gazed across the green. *I hope they didn't go for Poa Annua. It'll need more water than we can spare in this drought.*

> Joe crouched down and ran his hand over the deep green blades. He was worried. *This might have been a mistake.* "I wonder how this will hold up during the tournament."

Here we know who said "I wonder…" There is a new paragraph

and an extra space above to cue the reader about the POV change.

In Romance genre, however, there often isn't a cue other than a paragraph change. But since Romance normally switches between only two people it's usually clear who's head you're supposed to be in.

In both Multiple and Omniscient, an author can be inside many heads. In my book—a generational saga—*The Gods of Arkhon,* I get inside at least a dozen. Keeping my cues clear is extremely complex but vitally important.

Excerpt Example

The Gods of Arkhon, Book One, the Prophecy, Anita Burns

Atrius stared at Syntalla as if he could will her to awaken. "Please don't leave me. I need you." Thinking he saw her eyelids flutter, he studied her face. Nothing. Only stillness. "Please." He held her hand again and squeezed. "Please come back."

* * *

Urias swept into the medical compound, yellow-and-black robes rustling as she approached the front desk. "I am Urias of Wyrix, here to see Syntalla and Atrius."

The receptionist seemed flustered. "Uh..I don't know. No one told me—"

"Young woman. This is urgent. Who is in charge here?"

The girl stared, open-mouthed.

"Young woman," she repeated. "Did you not understand what I said? This is important."

"Um...I was told...just a minute... I'll see."

Is this girl mentally impaired? Urias crossed her arms and vowed to give the receptionist three seconds before she resorted to mind manipulation.

Multiple and Omniscient—Differences

In Multiple, the narrator does NOT know what's happening outside the awareness of the characters but is free to switch among them. The writer can be in Joe's head, Sam's head, the gardener's, Joe's mom's, Sam's wife's, but you can't tell about anything that's happening to people, places, and things the characters are not aware of.

What Not To Do in Multiple

> Sam inspected the grass on the course. "I haven't seen this kind before." Maybe they put in a new type. Looks good, but will it be strong enough?
>
> Meanwhile, a few yards away, the microwave in the clubhouse was rigged to a bomb and about to explode.
>
> Joe crouched down and ran his hand over the stiff blades. "I wonder how this will hold up during the tournament?" *I'll guess we'll just have to wait and find out.*

Sam and Joe are unaware of the bomb so it shouldn't be included in the scene. This is an example of author intrusion. To fix the problem, make one or both of the characters suspicious that something is wrong and then investigate, or become aware that there is a problem by having them, perhaps, walk into the clubhouse just as the microwave is about to blow.

Reworked

> Joe watched with interest as Sam inspected the grass on the course. "I haven't seen this kind before," said Sam.
>
> Joe crouched down and ran his hand over the stiff blades. "I wonder how this will hold up during the tournament? I guess we'll just have to wait and see."

He stood. "I'm ready for a rest before we open the course. "Coffee?" He headed for the club house.

"Sure," said Sam as he followed Joe.

Inside, Joe smelled something odd. "What's that?" A bright light caught his attention. He didn't know exactly what was going on but his old military training kicked in and he screamed, "Run!" He grabbed Sam's arm. "We need to get outta here, fast!"

They dove through the door and ran down the hill but not quick enough. The impact of the ear-splitting explosion pushed them to the ground and pelted them with debris.

Because the correct POV character, Joe, is now aware of the bomb, it can be included in the scene. Another way to handle this is to have the explosion happen without warning. Then they see, hear, and feel it.

Omniscient

In Omniscient, the narrator is like a god. He/she knows everything and can describe what's happening and see inside the thoughts and emotions of every character.

Comments on events unseen by the characters can be described in Omniscient. Some call this the "Meanwhile, Back at the Ranch"—style.

However, it is still important to demarcate a switch, or the unknown event described can confuse the reader.

Just as with Third Person Multiple, don't get into more than one head at a time. Doing that is called "head-hopping."

Many writers and writing professionals have differing opinions about what constitutes head-hopping and whether it's okay to do it or not. It can become confusing but if you stick with one POV per scene, you're on safe ground.

If you decide to use more than one POV per scene, it's best to cue a change in whose head you are writing from with by a scene-break mark of some kind—extra blank line, asterisks, hashtag, etc. Start the paragraph of the new POV character with his/her name so the reader isn't confused about who's talking, thinking, or acting.

Remember, though, that Romance is often an exception. It is common for this genre to use Third Person Multiple without cues (except for a paragraph break) and move fluidly between the two main protagonists (usually the hero and heroine).

Example Excerpt: Omniscient Romance

Shades of Gray, Amanda Ashley

> Marisa nodded, enchanted by his voice. Never had she heard anything like it: low, mellifluous. An angel's voice.
>
> Grigori studied the woman for a moment, noting that she was quite lovely. Her shoulder-length hair was dark brown with a slight curl; her eyes were bright and green, like fine-quality emeralds. . .

Note that Ashley starts each paragraph with the POV character's name, which can become monotonous if over used.

Example: Third Person Omniscient

> With the prom coming up, Jefferson High buzzed with activity. Teachers dreaded the event but the students radiated excitement. The town's formal shop had almost sold out of dresses and it was getting harder for boys to find a rental tux that didn't look like something from a wedding-singer gig. So, many students drove to Bailor's Corner, a town only a few miles over, to find their prom clothes.
>
> Anna was nervous. She had her dress but no date.

> She liked Tim but was afraid to ask him to go with
> her. What if he turns me down? He's so popular. Why
> would he want to go with me?
>
> Sitting in his car, Tim fretted. I want to ask Anna to
> the prom but she's so beautiful. I'm sure she already
> has a date.

The author wrote about the town and the students. For some editors, this would be seen as author intrusion. For others, it's a hallmark of Third Person Omniscient.

The description of the town and the students, etc. does not come from the observations, summations, or thoughts of either character. That's what makes it different from Third Person Multiple.

Omniscient and Multiple POV can be difficult to master. Some writers, however, seem to find these to be easy and natural. It's up to you if you want to use them. I would suggest, however, that you take courses and read up on the differences between Omniscient and Multiple POVs, and on head-hopping.

Personally, I rarely use more than one POV within a scene. When I do, the cue is a scene-break mark of three asterisks. Usually, an entire scene or chapter is in one POV.

If you'd like to join the fray and read more on the debate:

Advancedfictionwriting.com

Thewritepractice.com

Writerunboxed.com

Third Person Omniscient POV is well-suited to complex plots and sagas where there are several main characters and a host of minor characters. It lends itself well to literary fiction, action, and epic storytelling; for example, *Lord of the Rings*, or *Dune*.

Third Person Omniscient lets you grow your characters over time and even generations.

Example Third Person Omniscient, two POVs in one scene

The scene-break space is the cue for the POV switch.

> Harry sat in his car, gazing at the old farm. It'd been neglected since his Aunt Sybel died in the fall of '09. So when he discovered that his uncle had died and left the place to him, Harry put city life behind and drove out to the Kansas homestead where he was born.
>
> The town folk were not happy about Harry coming home. He'd left under suspicious circumstances. Many thought he was behind the mysterious death of his aunt. But the mayor encouraged them all to put on a welcoming face and let the dice fall where they may.
>
> He stepped onto the dirt and gravel driveway, shaded his eyes with a hand and peered at the fields. The acres of sunflowers, nearly choked with weeds, seemed to cry out for help.
>
> * * *
>
> John, the old caretaker watched Harry from behind the rusty screen-door as the tall, forty-ish man dressed in a suit and tie climbed out of his sleek sports car and scanned the farm. *I does what I can, me bein' the only one here an' all.*
>
> John's hand lingered on the screen door handle. He was about to walk out and greet his employer's nephew but changed his mind and took a step back into the darkness of the house. *I hope he ain't thinkin' a puttin' me out to pasture. From the looks of him, he's goin' ta need my help.*

Third Person Limited

Here the author knows only the thoughts and feelings of one character. Hemingway's, *For Whom the Bell Tolls*, and *Jurassic Park* by Michael Crichton are good examples of Third Person Limited POV.

Many believe Third Person Limited creates a more intimate relationship between the reader and the main character because we are experiencing the story through him/her at all times. It's a good choice if you have only one main character and your plot is linear with no side stories.

Example: Third Person Limited:

> Harry sat in his car, gazing at the old farm. It'd been neglected since his Aunt Sybel died in the fall of '09. So, when the call came that his uncle had died and left the place to him, Harry put city life behind and drove out to the Kansas homestead where he had been born.
>
> The wide, dirt driveway looked the same and the rambling farmhouse hadn't changed much, except for needing a new coat of paint. Chickens still roamed free, clucking and scratching in the dirt for a tasty snack.
>
> He stepped out of the car, shaded his eyes with a hand to gaze at the fields. The acres of sunflowers, nearly choked with weeds, seemed to cry out for help.
>
> He turned toward the house. A movement behind the rusty screen door caught his attention. *It's probably the old caretaker, John, scrutinizing me.* He started toward the weathered front porch steps. *I hope he doesn't think I'm going to put him out to pasture. I'll need all the help he can give me to bring the place back to life.*

Third Person Objective

This is the least popular of the third person POV. A narrator tells the story as an observer. There are no references to thoughts or emotions. Objective is written as a report. The narrator is like a video camera. Only what is seen and heard can be described.

This POV is a good exercise in learning how to show feelings instead of telling about them.

Example: Third Person Objective

> Marsha howled with laughter. "Surely you're joking?"
>
> Sharon's eyes grew wide. She sniffed and folded her tear-stained handkerchief. "I don't think you understand. It really happened. How could I joke about something like that?"
>
> Moving closer to the door, Marsha slapped her forehead. "I'm leaving now." She shook her head and glanced back at Marsha then left.

There are no references to emotions or internal thought—only a scene describing the action and dialogue. The emotions are known only through inference from the action.

The drawback to this POV is that it lacks intimacy. We never get inside anyone's head. It's difficult to write without slipping into a monologue of telling. Showing through action and dialogue without referring to emotions is tough. In the example above, it would not be Third Person Objective if the text said, "Pained by her friend's grief, she slapped her forehead…." You would have showed Marsha's emotions, and that she knew Sharon's emotions.

This is a rare POV for books. It's mostly used by a few intrepid short story authors; one book written in Third Person Objective is: *Blood Meridian: Or the Evening Redness in the West*, Cormac McCarthy.

Example: Third Person, Objective, Present Tense (See Chapter 3. Verb Tense)

Charlotte's Web, E . B. White

The goose shouted to the nearest cow that Wilbur
was free, and soon all the cows knew. Then one of the
cows told one of the sheep, and soon all the sheep
knew. The lambs learned about it from their mothers.
The horses, in their stalls in the barn, pricked up their
ears when they heard the goose hollering; and soon
the horses had caught on to what was happening.

As a beginner, this is probably not the style to use. Learn your craft first, then experiment with more obscure, complex POV.

However, if you're one who thrives on challenge and want to venture from the easiest POV—Third Person Limited—read, read, read. Then practice, practice, practice. Learn from seminars, tutorials, workshops, and courses. Get feedback from experienced writers and editors. Who knows, you might uncover a talent you never knew you had.

.3.

Verb Tense—Back to the Future?

When writing your book, you will probably use more than one verb tense. Third Person and usually First Person fiction are most often written in the past tense for narration and tags and in present tense for the dialogue.

Example 1

>   1. "Why do you believe that?" Lisa asked
>
>   2. "Why did I even listen to you?" She asked.

Number 2 asked the character's present about her past.

Example 2

>   James turned and looked out the window. Lisa's reflection showed in the glass. "We are at a turning point in the investigation. I can't give up now."
>
>   Lisa dropped her gaze to the floor. "I understand. I'm just worried about you, that's all."

Past Tense

Written as if the narrator is telling a story that has already happened.

Example

A horse walked into a bar.

The bartender turned to him and said, "Why the long face?"

Present Tense

Written as if the story is being told from the present. We move along with the character(s) as the story unfolds in real time.

Example

A horse walks into a bar.

The bartender turns to him and says, "Why the long face?

Future Tense

I researched books written in future tense and read excerpts from each one I could find. They all turned out to actually be written in present tense. As far as I know, there are no books written completely in future tense. Use Future mostly in dialogue.

Example 1

A horse will shortly go into a bar. The bartender is going to say, "Hey, why the long face?"

Example 2

Laura will stare at the woman in front of her. *Can she really tell my future?*

Madam Zarina will look up from her crystal ball and say, "I'm going to tell you something you will find shocking."

Past Perfect

Past Perfect is used when you are writing about something that happened in the past before something else in the past.

Examples

1. Susan knew her way around Cairo because she'd been there three times before.
2. When I got home from work, my wife had left dinner in the refrigerator.
3. If I'd known you were coming I'd have baked you a cake.

Use past perfect when you are narrating something a character is remembering or something you want to show as having happened earlier.

Mixing Tenses

If you are using past or present tense, be consistent. Mixing them inappropriately causes confusion and shows that you don't have a basic grasp on writing.

What NOT To Do

I wanted to shop for shoes so I drive to the mall.

There are two verb tenses in that sentence: "wanted" and "drive." They don't match. The first one is past tense. The second one is present tense.

Reworked

I wanted to shop for shoes so I drove to the mall. (past tense)

I want to shop for shoes, so I'm driving to the mall.

(present tense)

 I will want to shop for shoes so I'll drive to the mall. (future tense)

Example Excerpt

Margo, Molly Dillon

Past Tense for narrative and Present Tense for dialogue and internal thought:

> Ignoring the greeting, Jennifer addressed the lawyer. "Can we get on with this, please?"
>
> With confusion, like dense fog, still lingering in the air, Margo walked over to the chairs around the table and sat down.
>
> "All right, let's proceed." For a moment, Peter looked down at the legal document on his desk. Then, hesitantly and with trembling hands, he picked it up. "We're gathered here today to read the Last Will and Testament of Kevin Christopher Blair.

TIP: Use past tense for narrative and things that happened in the past. Use present tense for characters' dialogue unless they talk about or describe the past. Use present tense if you write a story in the present (usually done in first or second person).

Voice

What is "Voice?"

Voice is the unique way you put words together and a reflection of your view of the world. According to *GrammarGirl.com.* "Voice is the distinct personality, style, or the point of view of any creative work, including writing. Voice is what talent show host, Simon Cowell talked about when he told "American Idol" contestants to make a song their own and not just do a note-for-note karaoke version."

Voice isn't style. According to Brian A. Klems, at *The Writer's Digest in his article, The Difference between Voice and Style in Writing* (September 14, 2012)*, says,* "Style is much broader than Voice. Some writers have a writing style that's very ornate— long, complex and with beautiful sentences, packed with metaphors and imagery (think Frank McCourt and John Irving). Others have a more straightforward style—sparse prose, simple sentences, and such.

Here's one way to think about it: WD [Writer's Digest] strives to have its articles fit a similar style—conversational yet straightforward. But each piece is written by a different author whose own Voice colors his/her particular article within the style. The continuity of the magazine stays intact, but each piece is still different."

Voice is something intangible and unique to each author. For many, it is one of the magical elements of writing. It is your Voice that gives your writing life, power, and energy. It shows that you loved what you wrote. Author Judy Green says in *How Bullets Saved My Life: Fun Ways to Teach Some Serious Writing Skills*,

> "Strong Voice is engaging to read. Energy and emotions charge the writing so that it is compelling and full of conviction. The writer's tone is interesting and presence is powerful. Readers "hear" personality in the writing. Even a war thriller can be written from a pacifist Voice.
>
> A weak Voice, on the other hand, creates a watered-down effect, where the writer seems indifferent to the subject or distanced from the audience. The writing is plain, and the author sounds monotonous, flat, or even bored. With a weak Voice, a writer loses the reader's emotional investment."

Finding your Voice isn't easily taught and when you do find it, you might not even know how it happened. The characters you create will have some element of you in them. Yes, even the antagonists will, in some way, reflect your world-view, your psyche. Even if you think a character is a reflection of someone else, that's only partly true. The people in our lives are a reflection of who we think they are. Sorry to go all "Psych 101" on you, but this isn't my opinion. It is a time-tested truth about the human experience. Famous psychiatrist C.G Jung wrote:

"Everything that irritates us about others can lead us to an understanding of ourselves."

In my book *The Gods of Arkhon, Book One*, I found it difficult to create antagonists. My world view is very much a peaceful one even though I have been described as a competitive, alpha woman. So, I dug into that deep assertive part of me and devised an organization bent on destroying all that the characters had struggled to build. But because of who I am, deep down, I couldn't have the "black hats" be evil through-and-through. I delved into their psyche to make them redeemable.

Example Excerpt

The Gods of Arkhon, Book Two, Weokka, Anita Burns

> Gripping the wing of a weathered gargo-carving that jutted from the railing like a hideous apparition, Ek-Tonis leaned out. *All I have to do is let go. No one would hear me fall. No one. It would finally be over. The pain—gone. The guilt—gone. Khamma satisfied.*
>
> He lifted one foot from the floor. The wind howled and pelted him with the first offerings of an icy rain. *It would be so easy—*

How you plot and pace your book can be a part of your Voice. It also reflects how you experience the world on a conscious and unconscious level. Your Voice will tend to repeat concepts, props, physical characteristics.

Have you written about more than one character with green eyes? Are your characters often among the "beautiful people?" Do you find roses in more than one scene? Are your characters yawning, stretching, rolling their eyes in multiple scenes?

In the first drafts of my books I inevitably had people smiling or yawning and stretching. At one point, I described several "flat rocks." Edit your work so that you don't repeat favorite phrases, actions, or scenes without destroying your unique Voice. Find another way of showing your character's boredom or the shape of the rocks if they are important to the story If not, leave them out. This will still be from your Voice, and it will stretch your creativity and enrich your writing.

One of the most important rules in my editing and ghost writing is using the authors' Voice. I look at language patterns, pacing, scene patterns and descriptions, I edited the biographical book *You're a Slut*, by Kimberly Clark. It was written from a dark place—child abuse. The author told her story of struggle to overcome the horrors of growing up. Throughout the book, she seemed to have hope that healing was possible. She demonstrated that friendship was important to her and that she had forgiven her abusive father and brother, and even her distant, cold mother. She was on a journey to heal from her past. Her language was simple and reflective. I kept that in mind when editing her rough manuscript.

Excerpt from *You're a Slut,* Kimberly Clark

He told me he wanted to marry me, but I know he only said that because he thought it was what I wanted to hear. Valoria said that Steve is a master manipulator and would say anything to get me to stay with him.

When I saw him before he left for a trip to Disney with his family, I told him we were moving too fast and that I didn't want to get married so soon. He seemed quite happy with that.

He always went along with whatever I said because he didn't want to lose me again. He wanted to keep his "side" thing."

Snow Crash, Neal Stephenson

> The Deliverator's car has enough potential energy packed into its batteries to fire a pound of bacon into the Asteroid Belt. Unlike a bimbo box or a Burb beater, the Deliverator's car unloads that power through gaping, gleaming, polished sphincters. When the Deliverator puts the hammer down, shit happens. You want to talk contact patches? Your car's tires have tiny contact patches, talk to the asphalt in four places the size of your tongue. The Deliverator's car has big sticky tires with contact patches the size of a fat lady's thighs. The Deliverator is in touch with the road, starts like a bad day, stops on a peseta.

Stephenson's Voice would be recognizable in any book.

Douglas Adams, most known for his breakout absurdity humor novel, *The Hitchhiker's Guide to the Galaxy*, has a distinct Voice:

Example Excerpt

The Hitchhiker's Guide to the Galaxy, Douglas Adams

> For instance, on the planet Earth, man had always assumed that he was more intelligent than dolphins because he had achieved so much—the wheel, New York, wars and so on—whilst all the dolphins had ever done was muck about in the water having a good time. But conversely, the dolphins had always believed that they were far more intelligent than man—for precisely the same reasons.

His book *The Restaurant at the End of the Universe* would be recognized as being written by Adams simply from his unique Voice.

Example Excerpt

The Restaurant at the End of the Universe, Douglas Adams

> It is known that there are an infinite number of

worlds, simply because there is an infinite amount of space for them to be in. However, not every one of them is inhabited. Therefore, there must be a finite number of inhabited worlds. Any finite number divided by infinity is as near to nothing as makes no odds, so the average population of all the planets in the Universe can be said to be zero. From this it follows that the population of the whole Universe is also zero, and that any people you may meet from time to time are merely the products of a deranged imagination.

Compare the following from spy/thriller novelists Tom Clancy and Robert Ludlum

Example Excerpt

Locked On, Tom Clancy

A pair of Black Sharks emerged from a predawn fog bank and shot through the moonless sky at two hundred knots, just ten meters above the hard earth of the valley floor. Together they raced through the dark in a tight, staggered formation with their outboard lights extinguished. They flew nap-of-the-earth, following a dry stream bed through the valley, skirting thirty kilometers to the northwest of Argvani, the nearest major village here in western Dagestan.

With its factual, clipped language, this has a tinge of Noir, Robert Ludlum's Voice seems more fluid:

Example Excerpt

The Bourne Identity, Robert Ludlum

The trawler plunged into the angry swells of the dark, furious sea like an awkward animal trying desperately to break out of an impenetrable swamp.

The waves rose to goliathan heights, crashing into the hull with the power of raw tonnage; the white sprays caught in the night sky cascaded downward over the deck under the force of the night wind. Everywhere there were the sounds of inanimate pain, wood straining against wood, ropes twisting, stretched to the breaking point. The animal was dying.

Two abrupt explosions pierced the sounds of the sea and the wind and the vessel's pain. They came from the dimly lit cabin that rose and fell with its host body. A man lunged out of the door grasping the railing with one hand, holding his stomach with the other.

Ludlum's voice is more descriptive. It has color and flow. You have a hint that this is a story about people. Where Clancy is more technical and matter-of-fact.

Your Voice will vary somewhat from genre to genre. The way I wrote this book is very different from the conversational Voice my memoir blog, Confessions of a Confetti Head: *Life Goes On Even When You Don't Expect it.*

Example Excerpt

Confessions of a Confetti-Head, Blog, Anita Burns

It's 7 a.m. and the house is quiet, well except for our new feline addition, Pumpkin, who is investigating every nook and cranny and every hanging and dangling thing she can in her ongoing fantasy that she's a wild jungle cat on the prowl. No throw-rug is safe. No pencil can escape. No bit of dust can hide from her eagle eye. Every ledge that is at least two inches wide has to be conquered and every open drawer is a cave to be explored.

I swore just a few months ago, "NO MORE CATS! I am *not* the little old cat lady!"

I love cats. In fact, I love all animals. Well, maybe that's not exactly true. I can't say that I've ever really warmed up to hyenas after my trip to the Houston Zoo on a hot, sticky summer day. If you've ever smelled a hyena, you know what I mean. Also, maybe warthogs aren't on my cuddly, lap list either. And since I am usually compelled to give three examples of anything I give examples for, I will add in camels. Having almost made the mistake of riding one in Egypt, I can say that camels are on bottom of my list of animals I would opt to share my life with.

Unsure of your Voice? If so, try the following exercise:

1. Describe yourself in adjectives. For example, are you snarky, fun, flirty, serious? Make a list of ten of them. Find any patterns?

2. Who is your intended audience? Thinking people or serious people? Adventurous people? Make a list of ten qualities of people you think would enjoy your book.

3. What do you like to read and/or watch? List your favorite books, movies, TV shows, blogs.

4. If you are in a critique group or hang out with other writers, ask them to describe your Voice.

5. When you write, is it fun, satisfying, exciting? Or is it work and drudgery? If it isn't enjoyable, you haven't found your Voice.

It may take some time for you to settle into your Voice, but keep writing. Your Voice will come out and then, the universe is yours to command.

.5.

Verb Tenses

Passive and Active Voice

As you learned in the previous chapter, Voice is the personality of writing that distinguishes the author's style. Voice is also a term used in the context of "Passive" or "Active" verbs.

What is Passive Voice?

Basically, passive voice is when the subject is the action. i.e. "The boy was bitten by the snake." shows the boy as the subject being bitten. It's grammatically correct, but doesn't carry the impact active voice does: "The snake bit the boy." The snake is the actor; "bit" is the action; the boy is the object of the action.

Passive voice has been demonized by writers and editors who claim it shouldn't be used because it distances the reader and often sounds formal, wordy, and stuffy.

Is it always wrong to use passive voice? That's the subject of much debate. In my opinion, it's best to eliminate it as much as possible if you can still maintain a good rhythm and flow in your writing.

Examples

> **Passive**: Tomato Soup was eaten by Joann at lunch.
>
> **Active**: Joann ate tomato soup at lunch.
>
> **Passive**: The cake was baked by Sharon
>
> **Active**: Sharon baked the cake.
>
> **Passive**: An episode of *Suds 'R' Us* will be watched by our family.
>
> **Active**: Our family will watch an episode of *Suds 'R' Us.*
>
> **Passive**: The tree was climbed by me in record time.
>
> **Active**: I climbed the tree in record time.
>
> **Passive**: The entire house was built by one company
>
> **Active**: One company built the entire house.
>
> **Passive**: The picture was painted by my father.
>
> **Active**: Father painted the picture.
>
> **Passive**: The project will be worked on every day by me.
>
> **Active**: I will work on the project every day.

Look for these words in your text: Am, By, Was, Is, Are, Were, Have been, Will have been, Being

Those are clues that you might be using passive voice. When you can, change to active voice by rewording.

Keep in mind that sometimes Passive Voice has a proper place in your writing, and the above listed words are not always used in a passive way. **For example:** "He passed by the Laundromat on his way to the store." There are instances when active voice might be awkward. **For example**, rewording "It was Tuesday," might sound strange.

Stephen King wrote about how much passive voice irks him

Excerpt Example, *A Memoir of the Craft*, Stephen King

.... I won't say there's no place for the passive ... [voice]. Suppose, for instance, a fellow dies in the kitchen but ends up somewhere else. **The body was carried from the kitchen and placed on the parlor sofa** is a fair way to put this, although "was carried" and "was placed" still irk the shit out of me. I accept them, but I don't embrace them.

What I would embrace is **Freddy and Myra carried the body out of the kitchen and laid it on the parlor sofa.** Why does the body have to be the subject of the sentence anyway? It's dead, for Christ's sake! Fuhgeddaboudit!....

To read his complete rant:

westga.edu/~jloicano/Stephen_King_Passive.pdf

When to Use Passive Voice

According to fantasy novelist, *Susan Leigh Noble,* who seems to disagree with Stephen King, there is a place for passive voice:

When who is doing the action is unknown: "The pistol was missing."

When the recipient of the action is more important than who did it: "John Kennedy was killed by Lee Harvey Oswald."

When describing a minor character through the main character's thoughts or dialogue: "Money was left to Joe by his grandfather."

Bottom Line?

Choose passive voice as little as possible. But if it seems to belong there, and rewording creates something wordy and awkward, you might just leave it.

. 6 .

Outliner or Pantser?

Once you have your genre and POV figured out, what then? You may have heard arguments for and against making an outline first.

Which is Better?

It depends on how you like to work. One thing I have found, though, is that using some kind of outline, even a loosely structured one, usually saves time. If you go by the seat of your pants (being a pantser) with an idea and just start writing, there will likely be more rewrites than if you'd outlined. Outlining is more efficient, even if you just sketch out your beginning, middle, and end.

I recommend, K.M. Weiland's book, *Outlining Your Novel: Map Your Way to Success* and *Rock your Plot* by Kathy Yardley.

Outlining Apps?

Thanks to the tech-gods, there are a variety of software apps designed to help you outline your novel. I've used a few but for me, they were a waste of energy. I tried StoryMill but spent more time operating the app than actually writing. Then, when I decided to go back and make a change, it became even more frustrating to muddle through the windows, tables, lists, etc. It was easier for me to just make a loose outline and work from my own system. Although StoryMill is a solid, low-cost app that is intuitive to use, I quit because, as with tomatoes, I like my home-grown version better.

There seems to be an endless supply of apps to help a novelist outline—Mind-Map, Snowflake, Draft, and more. Here are a few offerings from *Writer's Digest*

> **Inspiration**: outlining, visual mapping, organizing, presentation manager
>
> **StoryMill:** Mac only, multi-level to track characters, scenes, and locations, timeline, snapshot editing
>
> **Story Weaver:** Windows only. An organic approach to story development.

One of the most popular writer's apps is Scriviner from *writersstore.com* It is a word processor and project management tool for writers of long documents such as novels, screenplays, and research papers.

A Case Against Outlining

According to *NY Book Editors,* if outlining helps you start writing, then use it. If, however, you find yourself locked into it and not exploring new avenues in your story, try something else. Just start writing. It doesn't even have to be at the beginning. You can start in the middle, the end, or anywhere in between. Let the writing guide you to what comes next. They advise to never tie yourself to limiting, "linear creation."

A Case For Outlining

Respected Christian book and screenplay editor, David A. Cathcart believes in outlining. According to him, outlining:

- helps you "beat writer's block"
- reduces chances of writing yourself into a corner
- speeds the writing process
- increases spontaneity
- reduces edits and rewrites.

Many writers believe outlining reduces the likelihood of a "sagging middle," so common when writers, especially beginning authors, don't plan ahead. The middle of the book just goes on and on, weighing down the story.

Advice? Use whatever system works best for you.

Outlining Without an App

Apps aren't a necessity. You can make one. After all, writers have outlined for longer than there have been computers.

Before starting an outline, think about your story. Jot down notes, ideas, thoughts, scenarios. If you're not a "jotter," use a voice recorder then transcribe later. Organize them any way you want—Notebook, MS Word, or whatever.

When you think you're ready to start your book, write a few lines on what the book is about. Include character(s) and the main problem or goal. If you can't do this, you probably haven't thought your story through enough.

When you are ready to write your outline, ask yourself some questions:

- What genre(s) do you think your book will fit into?
- What POV will you be using?
- Who is/are your main character(s)? Write a short and bio of them.
- What is the problem, challenge, or mystery that needs to be resolved, overcome, or solved?
- Why is the above important? What is at stake?
- What t can get in the way of the problem, etc?
- What time period is your book taking place in?

List some of the events that will take your character toward resolution, transformation, or triumph. Write a sketch of the scenes, including what purpose each one serves, who is in the scenes, where they are, what happens, what does each scene accomplish, and whose POV the scenes are from.

Take a look at your scenes. Reorder them if it seems to create a better flow. Add more if needed. Remove scenes that don't fit.

Step back and take a look at what you have. If you're happy with your outline, start filling in the blanks. Remember to keep your options open. Once you begin your story, you might find that it needs to go in a different direction, the characters need to change, or you need to add more tension, etc. Be ready for your book to surprise you.

As you write you will find—outline or no—that the characters seem to take on a life of their own. You may plan what they will do or where how they will handle a situation, but as you write, something different and even better might emerge.

.7.

Writing in Three Acts

As with plays and movies, books generally have three main acts. Although there are other systems that use more divisions, the three-act system has stood the test of time and is an excellent way to structure engaging stories.

Aristotle proposed, in 335 BCE, that "A whole is what has a beginning and middle and end." So, from ancient times—where Greek Tragedy theater reigned supreme—to modern cinema and literature, the 3-act system remains the gold standard of plotting a good story.

How a Three-Act Story Might be Played Out.

Act 1

- Set the scene
- Introduce the main character(s)
- Get the reader to care about the main character.
- Reveal the problem.
- Show characters in their "normal" setting.
- Create an inciting event that changes the life or direction of the main character. This can be

something unforeseen or unsettling. The main character could resist the change but be forced into it by circumstances beyond his/her expectation. He/she could go willingly but have mixed emotions or unrealistic expectations that could end in failure.

Act 2

- The main character faces great odds and huge challenges. He/she nearly fails.
- The goal becomes more complicated as other characters get involved or new challenges arise.
- Emotion runs high as the main character shifts into action and resolve to succeed.

Act 3

- The hero/heroine has a "moment of truth." He/she must transform something in him/herself in order to succeed.
- Challenge after challenge is nearly met only to be lost at the last minute.
- There is doubt whether there will be success or failure.
- A point of no return makes the hero/heroine nearly give up.
- At the last moment, there is a rising up with new vigor and resolve to defeat the opponent. The main character digs deep, transforms, and defeats the antagonist (or not).

There is a winding down with conclusion, emotional reactions, renewed hope, and/or philosophical resignation/understanding.

You can find dozens of guides in print and in eBook format

that will help you through this important subject.

Recommended reading: *Rock Your Plot*, Cathy Yardley

Structuring Your Novel, K.M. Weiland.

For an excellent breakdown of the three acts in The Wizard of Oz, I recommend, *Write Good or Die: Survival Tips for the 21st Century,* Edited by Scott Nicholson. It's a free ebook from *Amazon.com.*

A good story, no matter what the genre, progresses on a curve. It starts with a question, goal, or problem. It ramps up as the protagonist struggles to answer the question, accomplish the goal, or solve the problem. How you tell this is up to you.

Joseph Campbell's most famous work, *The Hero with the Thousand Faces*, spells out the plot used for centuries to captivate readers. This book has sold millions of copies and influenced countless writers over the decades.

The usual hero adventure begins with someone from whom something has been taken, or who feels there is something lacking in the normal experience available or permitted to the members of society. The person then takes off on a series of adventures beyond the ordinary, either to recover what has been lost or to discover some life-giving elixir. It's usually a cycle, a coming and a returning.

A Three-Act Analysis of Star Wars, A New Hope

Since George Lucas and Joseph Campbell were friends, I thought analyzing the plot of Star Wars would be a fun choice.

Act 1

> *Set the Scene*: The space ships. A battle. Darth Vader striding on board after victory.
>
> *Reveal the problem:* Darth Vader didn't get the item he

came for. It is important to retrieve it.

Introduce the main character (hero): Luke Skywalker lives on a farm with his aunt and uncle but dreams of being a pilot.

Show him in his "normal" world: The vaporator farm.

Get the Reader to care for the main character: He is an orphan and dreams of getting off the farm and becoming a pilot. There is a secret about his life that his aunt and uncle have not revealed to him.

Inciting event: After buying two droids, Luke discovers a secret message in one of them. This droid, R2D2, escaped the battleship in the first scene with protocol droid C3PO, and set out in search for the recipient of the message— Obi Wan. Luke and the other droid go after it. He meets Obi-Wan. While he's gone, Storm Troopers kill his aunt and uncle. Luke is thrown into the adventure—helping Obi-Wan defeat the Empire.

Act 2

The hero faces great odds and challenges: Luke faces challenges in the space port Mos Eisley, Imperial forces try to stop them from leaving the planet with Han Solo in his ship, the Millenium Falcon.

They discover the planet they were going to has been blown to bits. They are caught in a tractor beam and brought aboard the Death Star where they learn that the woman who created and placed the message in R2D2 is on board as a prisoner, due to be executed. The message contains plans on how to blow up the Death Star.

The goal seems out of reach and becomes more

complicated as Luke, Han, and Chewbacca attempt to rescue Princess Leia. Getting off the Death Star seems impossible. The Empire retaliates. Luke faces his first major setback— the death of Obi-Wan Kenobi at the hands of the evil Sith Lord, Darth Vader.

The hero needs to find a way to succeed: After a heroic battle, the hero(es) and heroine escape and set off to deliver the plans to the Rebel Alliance.

Emotions run high and the hero shifts into action and resolve: Luke vows to do what must be done in order to defeat the Empire.

Act 3

Moment of Truth: The hero(es) and heroine discover that the only way to destroy the Death Star is by dropping an energy cannonball down a small shaft. This won't be easy because the Star is heavily armed and protected. At this point, Luke considers himself just one of the guys rather than the hero. Things are not looking good for the Rebel Alliance.

Challenge after challenge: A seemingly impossible battle in space to get one of the tie-fighters in place to deliver the bomb. After the pilot that Luke was supporting is destroyed, the responsibility to destroy the Death Star falls on his shoulders. He tries once and fails. After nearly being blown to bits himself, Han Solo shows up and saves the day by protecting Luke's ship.

The hero doubts and comes to a point of no return: He's alone. He has failed. The enemy surrounds him. He's been hit. Should he retreat?

Transformation: Luke transforms into the hero by hearing the voice of his dead mentor, Obi Wan Kenobi, "Use the Force, Luke."

Last moment of resolve to defeat the opponent: Luke turns off his guidance system and follows the force. He fires and succeeds.

Winding down, conclusions, emotional reactions, renewed hope: Pomp and circumstance ceremony. Droids clean and shiny. Parade. Awards. Accolades.

Exercise

Read a classic book, then a contemporary book and note how the authors use the three acts. For free copies of classic, public domain books*: https://www.gutenberg.org*

8.

Out of the Starting Gate

Staring at the Blank Screen—How to Write a Great First Page

You may have outlined in detail, worked out the plot lines, chapters, and ending. You may have simply scribbled ideas on sticky notes and put them in some kind of order. Or you could have an idea in your head and no outline at all. Whatever prep you did or didn't do, eventually, you have to write that first page, the window to the rest of your book, the page that many others will use to decide whether to buy your work or not. Don't let fingers break out into a cold sweat. With a few guidelines, you can be happily typing an opening scene that will have potential readers wanting more.

Setting the Scene

Although it's important to give readers an idea of the where and when of the story in the first chapter, be brief. Unless it's important to the story, don't begin your book with long scene-setting or in-depth background information. It's a rare author who can pull this off. James Michener always starts his books with a detailed history of the area. In *Hawaii*, he began with the formation of the Hawaiian Islands millions of years ago. But only an extremely skilled author can do this well. It's been argued that Michener uses the actual place as the main character in his books—another difficult feat that requires advanced skills.

Before the age of movies and television, long scene-setting in fiction was perfectly acceptable. Today, it's best to get into the meat of the story as soon as possible. Reading even several paragraphs of where and when and maybe why has our eyes skimming the words or our fingers flipping through pages.

Example Excerpt

*War of the World*s, by H.G. Wells, published 1898

Genre: Science Fiction - What Not to do.

POV: First Person.

> No one would have believed in the last years of the nineteenth century that this world was being watched keenly and closely by intelligences greater than man's and yet as mortal as his own; that as men busied themselves about their various concerns they were scrutinized and studied, perhaps almost as narrowly as a man with a microscope might scrutinize the transient creatures that swarm and multiply in a drop of water.

> With infinite complacency men went to and fro over this globe about their little affairs, serene in their assurance of their empire over matter. It is possible that the infusoria under the microscope do the same.

> No one gave a thought to the older worlds of space as sources of human danger, or thought of them only to dismiss the idea of life upon them as impossible or improbable.

> It is curious to recall some of the mental habits of
> those departed days. At most terrestrial men fancied
> there might be other men upon Mars, perhaps
> inferior to themselves and ready to welcome a
> missionary enterprise. Yet across the gulf of space,
> minds that are to our minds as ours are to those of
> the beasts that perish, intellects vast and cool and
> unsympathetic, regarded this earth with envious
> eyes, and slowly and surely drew their plans against
> us. And early in the twentieth century came the great
> disillusionment. The planet Mars....

After this setup, Wells went on at length about what science then believed about Mars. This may be historically interesting but today's reader would prefer to have the story to begin with an inciting incident and read the important details as dialogue or in threads woven throughout later chapters.

TRIVIA NOTE

The War of the Worlds did not cause the infamous panic when Orson Wells presented it as an enactment on the radio in 1938. It was propaganda perpetuated by the newspaper industry.

Exercise

Read *War of the Worlds*. How would you begin this novel? Watch one of the movies made from the book. How does it begin?

Example

An engaging first page that sets a scene

When Dreams Take Flight, Judith McAllister

Genre: Historical Fiction

POV: Third Person Multiple

Chapter 1, after the Prologue:

Rose Sullivan stared down at the test paper on

the desk in front of her, at the blank lines below
the printed words: I'm applying to serve with the
Women's Air Force Service Pilots (WASP) because...

Biting her lip, she glanced at the wall clock. It was
hot in the flight briefing room and so quiet, she could
hear the tick of the second hand as it methodically
gobbled up what little time was left. The math test
had been a snap—but essay? She hadn't counted
on that. In high school, she'd had enough trouble
scribbling book reports and an annual paper on What
I Did Last Summer. Cap was right—there was more to
qualifying for the WASP than being a hot-shot aviator.

Rose stole a peek through the open doorway. Cap
slumped in a folding chair in the hallway, brooding
like a mother hen. She'd parked her lanky frame there
when Rose turned in her paperwork this morning—
application, pilot's license, birth certificate, academic
records, and a signed disclaimer that assured the
Army Air Force she wouldn't hold the government
responsible if she slammed an AT6 prop-first into a
mountain.

Cap had sat there, legs crossed, as she whizzed
through the math test.

Full of confidence at that point, Rose had given her
a sly thumbs-up. But now...I'm goint go be one of that
ninety-five percent, she thought. I'm goint to wash
out before I even climb into a military cockpit.

Although there is no dialogue above, the author paints an
intriguing picture that has the reader wondering about what is
going on and what will happen next. Building expectation and
creating scenes that ask questions is a way to engage the reader.

If scene-setting is important to the story, be brief and make it
from the character's POV or put it in a prologue. Prologues are
not common in genre books, but literary novels often use them
to set the scene or tell back-story.

Example 1

First chapter opening with too much detail and back-story.

In the kitchen, Sam slumped on the blue and white, hand-carved, ladderback wooden chair—one of six in the set. Just after they moved into this house on Mission Avenue, one of the chair legs broke when his uncle Verne landed his generous backside on it with overly zealous gusto.

Uncle Verne had passed away the year before. Sam hadn't gone to his funeral that his Aunt Gertrude had spend thousands on. He hated the smell of funeral flowers. Aunt Gertrude never forgave him.

Sam propped his hand-beaded-moccasined feet on the cherry-wood table his mother had given them as a wedding present. His mother was like that. She always gave the best. Just last week she gave cousin Kimberly a set of antique brocade drapes for a birthday gift.

Bluebirds and robins chirped outside in the spring air. Mostly their nests were in the old oak tree in the front yard. That oak had to be at least a century old.

The sound of a coffee-maker gurgling water into the filter full of dark roast decaf grounds sounded in the background.

Sam loved New Hampshire this time of year—much better than when they lived in New Mexico. He remembered his days in that state and shuddered. That's where he met Bess. It was at the Mercado. They had both wanted the same set of hand-blown, cobalt blue dishes. She told him she'd cut her hand that morning and was hesitant to hold a plate up to the light because she thought her bandaged fingers might make her drop the dish.

One look at her deep green eyes and he gave in. The dishes were hers. He would have given her the world if she'd asked. He sighed. *My life is in the toilet and I don't know what to do about it. Is there any hope that Bess will come back to me?*

Reworked

In the kitchen, Sam slumped in a chair, his mocassined feet propped on the table. Birds chirping outside and the gurgling coffee-maker on the counter only made him feel more miserable. "What gives them the right to be so cheery?" he grumbled. *My life is in the toilet and I don't know what to do about it. Is there any hope that Bess will come back to me?*

Or a slightly longer version

Sam slumped on the ladderback kitchen chair. He propped his moccasin-clad feet on the table his mother had given them as a wedding present.

Birds chirping outside and the gurgling coffee-maker on the counter only made him feel more miserable. "What gives them the right to be so cheery?" he grumbled.

He remembered the day he met Bess. It was at the Mercado in New Mexico. They had both wanted the same set of hand-blown, cobalt blue dishes.

One look at her deep green eyes and he gave in. The dishes were hers. He would have given her the world if she'd asked.

He sighed. *My life is in the toilet and I don't know what to do about it. Is there any hope that Bess will come back to me?*

Where he lives could be included if it's important for the reader to know. How he met Bess and the Mercado incident in New Mexico can be revealed in later paragraphs and scenes.

Bring in your protagonist and give an indication of what your book is about as soon as possible.

Introduce at least a hint of a conflict or an obstacle the character will be dealing with.

A rambling first chapter has readers wondering where your story is going. They might give up before you get to the point.

A Good Opening

Example Excerpt

Frankie, Molly Dillon

Genre: Mystery

POV: Third Person Multiple

> Frankie Poretti loped downstairs to fix himself a peanut butter and jelly sandwich and get a glass of milk. He'd aced his freshman history exam today and was feelin' good.
>
> Flopping down on the couch in the family room, he switched on the TV and had just begun to channel surf when a blond reporter standing in front of a familiar building caught his attention.
>
> "We interrupt our regular programming for late-breaking news. A car owned by Mafia leader Angelo Poretti was blown up about an hour ago as the notorious North Side Chicago Don prepared to drive away from Saint Anthony's Church." She turned and pointed to the building behind her.
>
> Frankie sat rigid. He couldn't seem to wrap his mind around what he'd just seen and heard. *This can't be real.*
>
> "According to Father Joseph Benedict, the family had come here to pick up Angelo Poretti's brother, Father Dominic Poretti. Also in the car were Angelo's wife, Jane, and his mother, Elizabeth. There were no survivors."
>
> "No! God! No! No! No!"

Notice how Dillon introduced the main character, Frankie, right away.

She showed him in his normal environment then immediately introduced an inciting event.

The drama of the situation sets up the "quest" for young Frankie, leading him toward a future life transformation.

Example Excerpt

The Color of Heaven, Julianne MacLean

Genre: Mystery

POV: First Person

> In this remarkable, complex world of ours, there
> are certain people who appear to lead charmed lives.
> They are blessed with natural beauty, have successful
> and fulfilling careers. They drive expensive cars, live
> in upscale neighborhoods, and are happily married
> to gorgeous and brilliant spouses. I was once one of
> those people. Or at least that's how I was perceived.

Here, Julianne Maclean sets the scene and the tone of the rest of the book. She was perceived as having everything, but is that the way she really felt? I'm thinking, not.

.9.

Characters

Good Guys, Bad Guys, Lovers

Although the characters in your book can be numerous, in the simplest genre novels, there are three main characters: Protagonist (the hero or heroine), Love Interest (Usually who the protagonist hooks up with), and the Antagonist (the villain).

Bring them in as soon as possible. The reader needs to have a reason to root for the hero and to hiss at the nemesis.

Love

What's a book without love—or at least a little passion? Romance isn't the only genre to include them. From mystery thrillers to children's books, love is often included in the story. In literature and film, there is usually a main character and at least one character that is termed the "love interest."

Depending on the genre, love interests can be introduced in the beginning, middle, or end of the book. In the simplest, most straight-forward Romance novel, for example, the love interest is most often introduced in the first or second chapter, even if the main character is clueless about where this relationship will lead. This juices up the question, "Will the hero and heroine find true love?"

Example Excerpt

Apache Flame, Madeline Baker

Genre: Western Romance

POV: Third Person Multiple

This is an intriguing beginning that opens up multiple possibilities for the plot.

> Chapter One, Canyon Creek, New Mexico 1869
>
> He was back.
>
> Alisha Faraday heard the news at least a dozen times in as many minutes. It seemed everyone who saw Mitch Garrett ride into town that rainy Friday in late April felt duty-bound to stop by the schoolhouse and tell her the news. Her first instinct was to run away just as fast and as far as she could.
>
> Hands shaking, she tried to concentrate on the test papers she had been grading, but it was no use. The words, whether neatly printed by Betsy Hazelwood or haphazardly scrawled by Bobby Moss, made no sense. How could she be expected to think about nouns and verbs and proper sentence structure when he was back?
>
> Oh, Lord, what would her father say?

Some Romance novels are more complex than others. Sometimes the author chooses to delay the introduction of a love interest. If this is the case, the part of the book that precedes the characters' meeting should have a story arch of its own.

In the famous gothic romance classic, *Jane Eyre*, 1847, Charlotte Bronte delays introducing the love interest until the second act of the book. Unlike many popular novels of its time, Jane Eyre has a complex plot with several subplots, each with a beginning, middle and end.

Three Act Outline

Act one starts with the orphaned Jane as an abused child, sent to the horrid boarding school, Lowood, headed by the shady religious fanatic Mr. Brocklehurst. In the school, Jane is humiliated and punished for being headstrong and branded a liar.

Jane loses her only friend to typhus. The one adult staff member who is kind to her gets married and leaves. She feels alone and abandoned.

Act two of the plot shows Jane grown up, a teacher in a much reformed school, the evil Mr. Brocklehurst, gone. She longs to see more of the world, and to expand her horizons, so she applies for a job as governess and is accepted. That's where she meets the intimidating Mr. Rochester (love interest #1), the master of the manor.

They are an unlikely couple, separated by a strict class system. Much has to be overcome and resolved before they can be together for the classic, happily-ever-after ending. On her wedding day, at the altar, their vows are interrupted by a stranger who claims that Mr. Rochester is already married—to an insane woman kept prisoner in one of the towers in the mansion. Jane has much to consider. Her desire to be with the man she loves clashes with her religious and moral values.

In Act three, Jane abandons Rochester on moral grounds and sets out on foot to roam the moors, trusting in providence to guide her to safety. She nearly starves to death before being rescued by a kind family, who takes her into their home and sets her on the road of independence as the local school teacher.

Jane undergoes more trials and emotional

dilemmas. She nearly accepts a marriage proposal
and the life of a missionary's wife (love interest
#2) but strange urges call her back to Thornefield,
where she is reunited with a broken and blinded Mr.
Rochester.

Exercise

Read Jane Eyre and analyze plot progression and how the book's opening draws you in—or not. Do you think that delaying the romance made the story more powerful and effective? Would you write it differently? How?

NOTE: Jane Eyre has been said to have changed how fiction was written. It contains social criticism, classist and feminism issues, sexuality, and religious dilemmas rarely touched on before. Even today this book is often required reading in schools and colleges.

Love and Passion in Noir Novels

"Noir" is a sub-genre, typified by Raymond Chandler's gritty detective stories from the mid 20th century. Contemporary Noir fiction is as popular as ever. A good example is Stieg Larsson's *The Girl with the Dragon Tattoo.*

Passion and lust was common in earlier Noir fiction. In recent novels, there is often more love than lust.

What distinguishes *Noir* from other novels that include strong love and passion is its gritty, dark, hardboiled style of writing.

In my opinion, the epitome of classic Noir is Raymond Chandler's, *The Big Sleep.* In this classic Noir book, love interest is introduced in the third chapter of the book. This isn't a romance novel but there is plenty of erotic attraction and tension between Marlowe and Vivian.

Example Excerpt

Chapter 3, *The Big Sleep*, Raymond Chandler, 1939

Genre: Mystery

POV: First Person

On a professional call as a private detective, Philip Marlow meets Vivian for the first time.

> I sat down on the edge of a deep, soft chair and looked at Mrs. Regan. She was worth a stare. She was trouble. She was stretched out on a modernistic chaise-lounge with her slippers off, so I stared at her legs in the sheerest silk stockings. They seemed to be arranged to stare at.
>
> They were visible to the knee and one of them well beyond. The knees were dimpled, not bony and sharp. The calves were beautiful, the ankles long and slim and with enough melodic line for a tone poem.
>
> She was tall and rangy and strong-looking. Her head was against an ivory satin cushion. Her hair was black and wiry and parted in the middle and she had the hot black eyes of the portrait in the hall. She had a good mouth and a good chin. There was a sulky droop to her lips and the lower lip was full.
>
> She had a drink. She took a swallow from it and gave me a cool, level stare over the rim of the glass.

Bad Guys

From evil geniuses to cowboys in black hats, the antagonists spice up the story. A plot without an antagonist often has readers yawning or worse putting the book aside. Because the struggle between antagonist and protagonist often drives the story, bring them both in as soon as possible.

There can be more than one antagonist, depending on the genre and the complexity of your plot. Some have redeeming qualities and may even turn into protagonists. Others are baddies through and through.

Examples of antagonists

- *Star Wars,* by George Lucas. The most notable antagonist is Luke's Darth Vader. But there is also Han Solo's Jabba the Hutt, and the over-arching Emperor—the evil Sith Lord.
- *Wizard of Oz*, by Frank Baum. The wicked witch is the antagonist preventing Dorothy from reaching the Emerald City.
- *Shogun,* by James Clavell, has several powerful antagonists, including Lord Ishido, Lord Yabu, and Father Martin Alvito.
- *We Need to Talk about Kevin,* by Lionel Shriver, A chilling novel. The antagonist is the main character—a sociopathic teenager who commits horrendous atrocities.
- *The Shining,* by Stephen King has complex antagonists, some of them are ghosts.
- *The Lion, the Witch, and the Wardrobe* from C.S. Lewis's *The Chronicles of Narnia* has the definitely evil Snow Queen.
- *The Old Man and the Sea* by Ernest Hemingway, a story where the sea itself is the antagonist.
- *When Dreams Take Flight,*Judith McAllister, a WWII story. Rose Sullivan faces the antagonist of traditional social attitudes about what it means to be a woman as she battles to become a first-rate pilot and recognized for being just as good as the men.

- No matter what genre, the antagonist has to be believable. In contemporary writing, the antagonist is rarely pure evil, except in children's literature—think, Cruella De Vil from *101 Dalmations*, or the stepmother in *Cinderella*.

Contemporary authors bring us into the minds and hearts of the antagonists or even create sympathy for their plight.

This is strikingly different from earlier writing that usually included a villain with no redeeming qualities.

In the Sherlock Holmes stories, for instance, no one is supposed to identify with or have sympathy for the evil genius,

Ian Flemming's James Bond books all feature an antagonist who evokes no sympathy—Moriarty.

These baddies are meant to be unrealistic, over-the-top characters. And yet, somehow, we still find them believable.

Femme Fatales of many old and new books are sometimes written with a sympathetic hand and sometimes not.

- *Farewell My Lovely,* Raymond Chandler, features the female siren, Helen Grayle, described as a conniving but alluring woman who moves through men like a bulldozer while she covers her sordid past as the flame-haired nightclub torch-singer, Velma Valentino. A tough past or not, there isn't a lot of empathy possible for her character.

- *The Devil Wears Prada,* by Lauren Weisberger, has Miranda Priestly, who seems to be cold, heartless, and more than a bit snobby. But what is eventually revealed about her, brings empathy and understanding for how she became so powerful and unsympathetic to the feelings of others.

Children's books tend to have antagonists of pure evil. In

the Harry Potter series, by J.K. Rowling, there is no doubt that the villain is evil to the core. There is no attempt to bring understanding or sympathy to the Voldamort character.

No one I know has ever sympathized with Captain Hook in J.M. Barrie's, *Peter Pan*, nor the Other Mother in *Coraline*

In the Romance genre, the antagonists are often each other. The classic "I hate you. I hate you. I love you," pits the two characters against each other until close to the end.

In Margaret Mitchell's *Gone With the Wind*, the American Civil war is the antagonist, as well as Scarlett acting as her own worst enemy.

Creating Characters with Depth

Your characters are the most important elements to make your story come alive. In visual media, they make the difference between a great show or movie and a documentary. I don't know about you, but no matter how interesting the topic is, I always nod off in documentaries.

Although it's important to describe major characters, they must be brought to life. Leave the "She was short and squat with sandy hair piled on her head like a haystack," for minor characters. Give a little more insight into the important people in your story.

Description only

> My father was tall and handsome. He had deep blue eyes and strong hands. His face was almost always covered by black whiskers that seemed to grow like weeds on his firm jaw. He dressed casually but in neat clothing and always had polished shoes.

Write descriptions that also say something about the character or mention something that shows personality.

A more Thorough Description

My father, a veteran of WWII, stood tall and lanky. His his easy smile and friendly way with words always put people at ease. Even the ever-present black whisker-shadow on his strong jaw didn't dim his handsome face. I remember that he was particular about what he wore. Until the 1960s, even though he was a truck mechanic, he always wore a collared shirt and tie to work.

This description gives a little insight into the man's character.

Watch out for Cliché Descriptions.

Be careful not to describe your characters in ways that have been used and reused too many times. "Clean-cut good looks" is an example. "She was a shrinking violet" is another. Think of creative ways to describe your character that are fresh and new.

Example Excerpt

The Gods of Arkhon, book Two, Weokka, Anita Burns

A woman unlike any he had ever seen stood to his left. His skin tingled at the sight of her and he felt rooted in place, unable to speak. Her hair, white as the sea foam he had seen as a child, floated in some unfelt breeze. Her eyes were deeply blue and her skin as light as the flowers that blossomed by the river in spring. She was tall—taller than any man in the village—and wore a robe seemingly spun from silvery spider webs that wafted around her radiant body in a graceful dance.

Make physical descriptions strong.

Instead of just saying that she had short hair, you might bring it more alive with an additional description.

Example

> Her hair framed her dimpled face in a cap of shining, auburn curls.

Example Excerpt

Seize the Lightning, Madeline Baker

> A faint shuffling sound preceded the old man's entrance into the living room. For all his years, Samuel Gray Bull looked like he was in pretty good shape. He was a little bent over, his long, black hair showed more iron than ebony, but his black eyes were as sharp as a skinning knife.

Character descriptions should be revealing.

An idiosyncratic movement or mannerism can show much. A tremor, limp, eye twitch, or cheek biting says a lot. Pick dominant features to describe. Sea-green eyes, Roman nose, a mouth that needed kissing, raw elbows and knuckles. These are things that bring up images to help the reader know your characters.

Include fragrances and odors, too. Our sense of smell creates strong emotions. Describing them in scenes creates a sensory banquet that brings them to life.

Without descriptions that reveal character, you have to resort to telling. Telling can be flat and uninteresting. Make your characters real instead of just cardboard cutouts.

Example Excerpt

Confessions of a Confetti Head--Peeling Potatoes for Jesus, Anita Burns

> There I stood, 18 years old, 5-foot, 4 inches tall and weighing almost 98 pounds, shaking in my rubber boots.

I stared at the *ginormous* table in front of me then at the three beefy women, one next to me, the others on the other side of the table.

These ladies looked like they spent their nights chugalugging cheap beer and filling their jaws with chewing tobacco.

Musty-smelling dust filled the already stale air of the cavernous factory. A CLANG and nerve-grating buzzer sounded. The platform I stood on shook beneath my boot-clad feet. Then with a booming roar, the tsunami of partially peeled potatoes rushed down the chute toward us.

We grabbed them and gouged out their eyes. We hacked at black, rotten spots, mold, insect damage, and anything else we didn't like then tossed them onto a downhill slide that chopped them into French fries.

The thick, pungent, and sticky smell coated the inside of my nostrils. The floor was spread with slime. The pockety, rackety, grindy noise of the machines crept into my head until I thought my brain would melt.

One of the women was shout-singing, over the din of rumble, creak, clang, and bang, "Doin' the work for Jesus. Making spuds for the Lo-orrd!"

Zillions of naked potatoes, like brown, spotted monsters kept racing toward us faster and faster. Visions of Lucille Ball at the candy factory loomed in my mind as I watched the three she-buffalos whittling away like beavers in a tree-felling contest. Stuff flew everywhere! Up my nose, in my face and hair, and down my shirt. The floor was slick with potato rot. AAAARRRRGGGHHH!!!!

Actions can also help readers get to know the character.

Is she a vagabond? Home body? How does she shop for shoes? Does she hike, jog, play tennis? Is knitting her passion? Give

your characters something to do that reveals a bit about who
they are.

Example

The novelty of being "Sadie, Married Lady" wore
off quickly and I realized what a mistake I'd made.
OMG!!!! I was trapped in Normalville!

Everything important was happening in San
Francisco! What was I doing in a small town, cleaning,
cooking, and putting up with my mother-in-law's
constant demand for grandchildren?

I wanted more from life. I didn't drive. Rick wouldn't
let me. I felt trapped. I couldn't get a job or go back
to school. Rick didn't want his wife working. Later,
after his grandmother gave him a "tongue-lashing,"
he grudgingly let me take a of part time job and enroll
in college.

One day, I decided enough was enough. The world
was passing me by. Shortly after watching the first
moon landing on a flickery black-and-white TV, I
vowed to "Get outta here and into the action." It was
a time of war protests, riots in Berkeley, the people
demanding to be Heard!

I bought a bus ticket to Frisco, and was on my way.
To what? I didn't know or care. Something would turn
up. It did.

When I got off at the bus station, a sylph-like young
woman with frizzy blond hair and gauzy, gypsy-esq
clothing, handed me a flower and said, "Peace and
Love." I was supposed to give her money, but instead,
I said, "I want to join the cause. Who can I talk to
about that?" She looked surprised, then grinned with
perfectly straight white teeth that set off her natural,
no make-up beauty. I was entranced. I wanted to be
her. Yeah, right. Like I could EVER be like that.

What does the above example tell you about the character that
isn't said?

Exercise

Write a short biography of all the important characters in your story—not to include the descriptions in your book but to help *you* get to know them. It good to know their background, hopes, wishes, fears, triumphs and failures. That way, when you describe them in your story, you have a feel for who they are and choosing what to reveal to your readers is easier.

Above all, have fun with your characters. Make them love, hate, cry, laugh. Give them life!

10.

Scene Breaks and Chapters

When I first started writing, I had no idea what the parameters were for a chapter. Were there rules about length, how to begin, how to end? What's the difference between a chapter and a scene?

I just started writing and ended chapters whenever it felt right. Although my organic style was comfortable, I soon discovered that it wasn't always working the way I wanted. I started some chapters that didn't draw readers in and ending some that didn't compel the reader to turn the page. I crammed scenes together in ways the resulted in confusion.

I was clueless about the structure of a book, especially about scenes. What is the best way to move from one scene to another?

Scene Breaks

When there is a change of scene, the reader has to have a signal that shows that there is a switch.

A scene break (marked with a cue) can be a change in POV within the same scene, a new scene that is closely tied to the previous one, or a small leap in time but related to the scene as a whole.

Example

A break in POV change within a scene

> Lily thought she had died and gone to heaven. "What a beautiful surprise." She looked at the wild flowers offered up by little Bobby. His eyes so bright and his smile so wide, she thought he would burst out laughing.
>
> "Happy birthday," he said with a giggle in his voice.
>
> *He must have just picked these off the hill out back. What a loving child he is.* Lilly wiped a tear from her eye as she held the flowers in one hand. "I'll just go and find a vase for these and put them in a special place.
>
> * * *
>
> Bobby felt relieved that his aunt Lilly was pleased. He'd wanted to give her roses but found out his $1.50 wouldn't buy even one. *These are better anyway.* He watched her place the bright orange, purple, and yellow flowers in a deep blue vase and sighed. *When I'm older, I'll get her all the roses in the universe!*

Notice that the change in POV from Lilly to Bobby is separated by ***. This is a common scene-break cue. You can also use #, an extra space between paragraphs, or any other symbol you choose. Just be consistent.

The change from Lilly to Bobby is within the same scene so it is not a good place for a chapter break.

Keep in mind, though, that chapter breaks are more subjective than scene breaks that are used to clarify who's POV you've jumped into.

Example

A minor scene change and small leap in time

Bobby felt relieved that his aunt Lilly was pleased. He'd wanted to give her roses but found out that his $1.50 wouldn't buy even one. *These are better anyway.* He watched her place the bright orange, purple, and yellow flowers in a deep blue vase and sighed. *When I'm older, I'll get her all the roses in the universe!*

* * *

"The flowers look good on the table, Auntie." Bobbie took a bite of the grilled cheese sandwich Lilly had prepared for him. It tasted like sunshine. Somewhere in the back of his mind, he remembered his mother holding him in his arms and walking through a field of daisies flooded with warm sunlight.

Chapters

A chapter is a scene or a collection of closely related scenes. When there is a notable change—time, place, POV, or turn in the plot—start a new chapter. A break of this kind emphasizes that the story is changing in a significant way.

I often ask students to think of it as being like taking a long road trip. You have a beginning, a destination, and a roadmap to follow. Along the way, you will travel through different terrains, towns, cities, maybe even different states. You could have some surprises and setbacks, detours, or trouble—flat tire, run out of gas, road work, accident, heavy rain or wind, or be stopped by a policeman for running a stop sign.

Some changes on your journey are easy and flow together. You travel a highway through farmland then into a small town that supplies the local farms. This might be two scenes in the same chapter.

You make a turn onto a major freeway or Interstate. Traffic is heavy and fast, taking you into a large city with tall buildings, wide streets, bustle, and noise. This might be a new chapter.

The road from the small town led you to the city, but they are so different, they seem unrelated.

You might leave the city and enter a long stretch of desert, or turn onto a mountain road that winds with twists and turns, then back into a different city or cross over a state line.

Eventually, you overcome each challenge or setback and reach your destination.

Starting a Chapter.

Starting the scene or chapter with an action, internal thought, or dialogue from the POV character avoids confusion by showing readers whose head they're supposed to be in.

This is only an issue for third person POV. If you're writing in First Person or Third Person Limited, there is only one head to be in, so it's not an issue. Just watch that you don't make mistakes in writing something the POV character couldn't possibly know.

#1 Starting with the non-POV character, wrong

Sara watched her newly adopted son, Tommy, as he played with the toy truck she'd given him.

"Thanks," beamed Tommy. "I love this." He knew then that he had found a permanent home.

"Sara watched," says that the POV is Sara's, but in the next paragraph, Tommy "...knew then that he'd found a permanent home." This is from Tommy's POV.

To make the scene work the second paragraph needs either a change in POV cue or a rework so the whole scene is from either

Sara or Tommy. Probably reworking it is the better choice since the paragraphs are so short.

Reworked: Starting with the POV character

Tommy zoomed the toy truck around the room, crashing it into his stack of blocks. He glanced over and saw his newly adopted mother watching him from the sofa. "Thanks, Mom," he beamed. "I love this." He knew then that he had found a permanent home.

#2 Starting with the non-POV character, wrong

Josh tapped the steering column and leaned forward to frown at the traffic in the hover-lanes. "I'm sure there has to be an alternate route." He glanced at Sylvia. "Look it up, will you?"

Sylvia sighed, She hated it when he made her navigate. *Will he ever learn to use the navbar himself?*

The above sample starts off with Josh. Even though there is no indication that we are in his POV—just his actions—we assume that Josh is going to be the POV character for this scene because the writer starts with "Josh tapped..."

Reworked: Starting with the POV character

Silvia watched Josh tap the steering column and eye the traffic in the hover lanes. She knew what was coming.

"I'm sure there has to be an alternate route," he said looking at her with a raised eyebrow. "Look it up, will you?"

She sighed. *I hate it when he makes me navigate. Will he ever learn to use the navbar himself?*

First person POV, wrong

> I stood at the door and scanned the dancers, frantically gyrating to the heavy beat of the music. *He's, here, somewhere, I know it.* After a few minutes, I headed for the bar to wait.
>
> Josh stood over the men's room sink, staring into the mirror and wondering if he really wanted to be there.

Although the "I" character might have guessed that Josh was in the bathroom, she couldn't have known that Josh was looking in the mirror and wondering. Even so, if she was guessing where he was, the text should have indicated that.

The second paragraph also changed POV from first to third.

Partially Reworked

> I stood at the door and scanned the dancers as they frantically gyrated to the heavy beat. *He's, here, somewhere, I know it.* After a few minutes, I headed for the bar to wait.
>
> Little did she know that Josh was standing over the men's room sink, staring into the mirror and wondering if he really wanted to be there.

The "Little did she know…" line fixes the POV tense error but now it is an author intrusion problem.

Reworked

> I stood at the door and scanned the dancers, frantically gyrating to the heavy beat. *Josh is here, somewhere, I know it—probably in the men's room.* After a few minutes, I headed for the bar to wait.
>
> "Hey," said Josh.
>
> I turned and there he was. Something in his eyes told me he was having second thoughts about being here.

Now, everything is from the 1st person's POV.

Ending Chapters with a Hook

The old adage, "Always leave 'em wanting more," certainly applies to fiction. Although the end of a chapter ties up some loose ends, resolves something, or creates a mini-ending for the scene, give the reader a reason to turn the page—a teaser. Raise doubt, elicit a question, or bring in a surprise of some kind that will have the reader wanting to find out what comes next.

Excerpt Example

The Gods of Arkhon, Book One, The Prophecy, Anita Burns
On the way home, the restlessness returned. Images of Synti and Herala made Atrius' conflicted feelings tumble. Shaking his head, he rubbed his eyes. *Get a grip, Ati boy. You just need to work.*

Something in the dark recesses of his mind warned him to be careful or his world could fall apart.

He pushed it aside.

The ending of this chapter shows that things might not be as secure as Atrius thinks. He's ignoring signals that warn of coming danger.

Excerpt Example

Margo, Molly Dillon

Genre: Mystery/Women's Fiction

POV: Third

The second week, they rented a car and drove to San Diego, taking in Sea World and the San Diego Zoo. One night, near the end of the trip, Bobby had exclaimed, "Know what I like best about this vacation? I get to pick every restaurant we eat in."

> Jeffrey grimaced. And Margo smiled as she
> remembered his retort. "And if I have to eat one more
> burger, young man, I am definitely going to barf!"
>
> Everyone giggled, and through the joy of it all,
> Margo had wondered what wonderful things fate had
> in store for her son in the years to come—wonderful
> hadn't exactly been the right word—fate it seemed,
> possessed a cruel streak.

Ending a chapter well raises the tension level. It keeps readers interested in the story and wanting to find out what is coming next. Is the bomb really going to go off in the space station? Will the hero discover that his sister is really his mother?

Chapters have varying degrees of suspense or relating to other chapters. Not every chapter has to end with a bang. Sometimes a good hook is thoughtful or raises a question. Endings should always reflect something that has come before to maintain continuity.

Excerpt Example

Margo, Molly Dillon

Genre: Mystery/Women's Fiction

POV: Third

From Chapter 17

> She began to tremble, not from the chilly, damp
> wind, but from the alarming realization that she was
> staring straight into the same dark eyes she had fallen
> in love with thirty-one years before. His black hair was
> streaked with gray, but the six-foot-two-inch frame
> was as solid as it had been at the age of sixteen.
>
> Wagging her tail, the excited dog danced around
> Margo—inside her soul, Margo jitterbugged right
> along with her. On this cold, rainy day in April, David
> Anderson had come back into her life. This was the
> secret, the lingering sense of mystery about the town
> of Belmar that she'd never been able to shake off—

serendipity in its purest form.

As her trembling eased, Margo felt the odd
sensation of being frozen—frozen in some kind of
cartoon-like time warp. She managed a smile, but the
only word which escaped from her numbed mouth
was, "Hi."

From chapter 18
It felt like an out-of-body experience, but the
"body" followed David into the house....

Dillon starts the next chapter by relating to the end of the previous one.

Don't just throw in a thought or action that has nothing to do with what happened in the chapters before or with what's to come. Chapters should link together like a chain even if an idea or plot point is partially skipped then brought back into the story line in order to build suspense. This is a common device in mystery thriller and spy novels. Eventually, though, everything is tied together.

Hooks entice, push, or pull us into reading further. In film, these are called "cliff hangers" from the old silent movie serials, *The Perils of Pauline.* Each installment would have Pauline clinging to a branch on a cliff or in an impossible situation with no way out in sight. The next installment would show how she managed to survive.

One of the most famous unintentional cliff hangers is from Arthur Conan Doyle's Sherlock Holmes book, *The Final Problem.* Doyle was tired of writing about the super sleuth and hoped that would be the end of it, so he killed Holmes in a final struggle to the death with Moriarty. The backlash of this decision surprised him. Over 20,000 readers canceled their subscriptions to *The Strand* (the magazine that published Sherlock's adventures) and people took to the streets wearing black armbands and veils.

Fan pressure was so strong that Doyle devised a way for Sherlock to have survived the plunge from the Reichenbach Falls and continued to write more adventures for Holmes.

Good Chapter Endings Can
  • goad and prompt readers to turn the page.
  • raise tension or conflict.
  • introduce new problems, situations, or characters.
  • reveal something new about a character.
  • reveal a new secret or complication.

Avoid ending chapters with someone going to bed unless it is to dream about something intriguing or it is a prelude to an important plot point.

Chapter endings should not resolve plot issues. They could resolve pieces of them but not answer all the questions.

The End of the Journey

The last chapter of the book needs to tie up loose ends, resolve all conflicts or issues, show who killed "Roger Rabbit," bring lovers together or split them apart permanently. The hero conquers the dragon, and the princess is saved. The bad guy is in prison and everyone lives happily ever after—or not.

The final chapter is about fulfillment and resolution but the road along the way holds all the fun and all the excitement.

.11.

Populating the Story

You might populate your story with a few characters or with hundreds. How you bring them into your book can make a big difference on whether a reader will continue or become frustrated and put the work down.

One major mistake is introducing too many characters at a time, especially in the first pages. This confuses people. It's hard to hold too many names and descriptions in our head when they are poured onto us in great crowds. A reader likes to savor and become familiar with each character before moving on to the next. Two or three people are fine but more than that is like moving along a reception line of people you don't know. Do you really remember all those names and faces?

Too Many Characters Introduced in a Scene

> Sara took a sip of her martini then glanced around the room, John stood on the other side of the bar talking to a pretty blond "Is that Julia?" *She's had some work done on her nose. And those boobs, hmmm. I hardly recognized her.*

Martha came up and tapped Sara on the shoulder. "Barry is here and he wants to talk as soon as possible. It's about the Istanbul job."

"I don't want to talk to Barry until Josh gets here. He has the details." She reached into her bag and retrieved her phone. "No message. I wonder what's keeping him? Could it be his sister, again? She's so needy."

Six characters in the first three paragraphs are too many. As the book continues, it's going to be difficult to remember who's who.

Reworked

Sara took a sip of her martini then glanced around the room. John stood on the other side of the bar talking to a pretty blond.

Martha came up and tapped Sara on the shoulder. "Barry is here and he wants to talk as soon as possible. It's about the Istanbul job."

"I don't want to talk to him until Josh gets here. He has the details." She reached into her bag and retrieved her phone. "No message. I wonder what's keeping him?

In the reworked version, we left out Julia, who can be introduced later.

Sometimes a scene will have multiple characters. Even if they are already known to the reader, how do you keep the scene clear and avoid confusion or awkwardness with too many he-said-she-said tags or endlessly repeating characters' names?

Putting in action tags and/or internal dialogue helps the reader remember the characters. If possible, it's best to avoid having more than three in a scene, or have multiple characters but limit the talking to just one or two.

Excerpt Example

The Gods of Arkhon, Book One, The Prophesy, Anita Burns.

POV: Third Person Multiple

Genre: Literary/Science Fiction

The scene POV is Atrius, the main character. He and his son, Bontiel, are in a tribal council meeting in a ceremonial hut. It is raining.

All the characters have been introduced in earlier chapters. "Tumoyot" is the tribal deity. The villagers believe Atrius is a minor god sent to them by Tumoyot.

> Inside, they sat around the fire with Turbok, Otruwa, Sisketo, and the six Elders. A draft pulled in the pungent odor of sodden ground that mingled with the smells of burning wood, steaming fur cloaks, and wet bodies.
>
> "So," said Turbok, "you have called us here. My heart says you are leaving our village. Is it true?"
>
> Atrius studied the men in the circle. Shock, dismay, and fear showed on their faces. "It is."
>
> "But why?" asked Sisketo. "Have we displeased Tumoyot?"
>
> "We have honored Sky Father's wishes in all things," said Hadepa'a. "Why would he take you from us?"
>
> Atrius opened his mouth to speak but shut it when Hadepa'a spoke again.
>
> "Is it because of what happened to Syntalla? That wasn't our doing."
>
> The elders all talked at once with a cacophony of concerns, questions, and defensive comments.
>
> Turbok shouted, "Stop! Let your god speak"
>
> The men fell silent.
>
> "We are leaving. It is true," said Atrius. "Tumoyot is greatly pleased with your people. You have done well in his eyes. He has told us that Turbok, Sisketo,

and Otruwa now carry the light of his heart. We are needed elsewhere."

Mouths agape, the Elders stared at the three chosen men.

Turbok lowered his gaze.

Sisketo sat straighter and glanced at each one in the circle.

Otruwa held his focus on Atrius. "We are ever grateful for the guidance and help you have given us."

Turbok gave a deep sigh. "You, Syntalla, and Bontiel are one with my spirit. Your absence will bring grief and sadness."

Sisketo sighed and nodded agreement.

"We honor your grief. It is the way of things," said Atrius. "Also, honor what we have given you. Continue to teach your children the ways of Tumayot. Be at peace. Think with goodness in your heart. Be strong. Be happy."

By using dialogue and interaction with the POV character, this scene, even with many players remains clear.

It's not always easy to choreograph characters in a scene but worth the effort so the story flow isn't interrupted. You don't want your reader thinking, "Who was he, again?" then having to flip or scroll back pages to find the character's introduction.

12

Describing Characters and Scenes

Describe your characters, but not down to the number of hairs on their arms.

It's important to let your readers know what your characters and environment look like but what you show should have a purpose and/or reveal something relevant. Too much description slows down the flow of the reader's experience and detracts from their immersion in the story.

Describe main characters in detail. With minor characters you can be brief.

Meet John Doe

In life, when we meet someone, unless we're like Sherlock Holmes, we don't scrutinize every tiny facet of their appearance. We notice certain things and form impressions of what they look like and who they are as a person. We will notice more about people potentially important in our lives than those we simply pass in the street or casually greet in a social or professional setting.

The depth of detail you describe needs to be based on the

importance of the character to the story. You can spread it out over a few paragraphs or pages or all at once. It depends on what is required for the scene.

Give the reader an overall impression of who this person is and what he/she looks like. If Ed is a potential antagonist, bring out the parts of his appearance that could be a tell. For instance, flinty eyes, a nervous twitch, or big, meaty hands. A potential love partner might have a different set of tells—deep, dark eyes, a winning smile, sensitive hands.

Descriptions are Important

When a character is introduced, the reader will form an internal image of him/her whether or not you give a description. It's annoying, for example, to have a certain image of a character as short, squat, and fat, only to be told later that he is towering over someone or thin as a rail. Help readers form an accurate picture of the character so that these kinds of surprises don't pull them out of the story as they struggle to reformulate their internal representations.

A Main Character Description that Falls Short

> Stu was the kind of guy you just wanted to punch in the nose. He was as disagreeable as the pigs on my grandfather's farm. *I think he must have had a fight to the death with a bar of soap and the soap lost.*

Although the above gives some insight into Stu's personality and personal hygiene, it tells us nothing about what he looks like.

Readers will fill in the gaps with their own imagination. This is fine as long as you never give a more detailed description that goes counter to the images in a reader's head.

Reworked

> Stu was the kind of guy you just wanted to punch in the nose. He was as disagreeable as the swine on my grandfather's farm. *I think he must have had a fight to the death with a bar of soap and the soap lost.*
>
> As I listened to him ranting on about the evils of government, his fat hands and little sausage fingers waved about in righteous indignation. His short, paunchy body was stuffed inside a white latex running suit that made him look more like a boiled kielbasa than a lawyer.
>
> Combined with his pudgy, turned up nose that barely separated little, squinty black eyes beneath a pink, bald head, he really did look like one of grandpa's pigs.

Now, there's no doubt about most of what Stu looks like.

NOTE: The genre also drives what kind of description to use. For example in Romance and Young Adult, describing clothing is often important.

For minor characters who won't be in the story more then once or twice, a simple height, coloring, and hair might suffice. Or, just an occupation could be sufficient. We don't need to know much about them. Give just enough to place them into the scene.

A Minor Character Description

Ida is the main character and has been described earlier. The Nurse is only in one scene.

> Ida sat in the doctor's waiting room, her nerves on edge. What's taking them so long?
>
> The door next to the reception desk swung open and a young nurse holding a clipboard stepped through. "Mrs. Russett?"
>
> The look on her pretty face told me it was bad

news. I followed her into the physician's office and stiffly sat down across from the doctor. He had his usual, no-nonsense face firmly in place.

"I'm sorry, Mrs. Russett. It looks like your husband will remain a vegetable."

Even with important characters, it is possible to go overboard with description. Although you need to give enough to hook the reader into the story, place, or character, too much detail slows us down and acts like speed bumps, taking us out of the experience.

Too Much Detail

POV: First Person. In this scene, the protagonist is describing Nicholas, who will play an important part in solving the mystery.

Nicholas was seven and a half inches over six feet tall. He was, as usual, freshly shaved with a few straggler-whiskers that had escaped his barber's razor. The five fingers on each hand were long and tapered, with only a slight curve of the little finger of his left hand, and always well-manicured. The wart on his left thumb stuck out like a tiny ear of Indian corn. He had a wide barrel chest that strained against his hand-made embroidered waistcoat that pulled the Chinese eight-millimeter pearl buttons against their stitched buttonholes. His dark purple, tailored velvet coat with black satin lapels that laid flat against his body, caught every flake of dandruff that fell from his long, stringy, white and grey hair. He hid his balding tête under an Italian-made beaver top-hat that he wore at a slight angle.

The regal expression of disdain he so obviously nurtured and practiced gave him an air of superiority, as he sniffed at me through a hooked nose speckled with large, blackened pores revealing thick bristly hairs not so neatly trimmed fringing his flared nostrils.

That's a lot of description. Maybe shortening would give a more engaging picture of Nicholas. Keep in mind that you don't have to have all the descriptions of a character lumped together. You can bring out details throughout the scene.

Reworked

Nicholas was tall. His fingers were long and tapered and always well-manicured, and the wart on his left thumb stuck out like a tiny ear of corn. His barrel chest strained at the embroidered waistcoat that pulled the pearl buttons against their buttonholes. His dark-purple velvet coat with black satin lapels caught every flake of dandruff that fell from his long, stringy, grey hair and he hid his balding tête under an Italian-made beaver top-hat.

The regal expression he so obviously nurtured gave him an air of superiority as he sniffed at me through a hooked nose speckled with large, blackened pores revealing thick bristly hairs, not so neatly trimmed, that fringed his flared nostrils.

How is the second description more appropriate? Would you write it differently? Some authors would slim the above down even more. What do you think? Should it be even less detailed?

Too Much Description

POV: Third person

Jay scanned the application. Stanley Fisher, born April 9, 1984. He looked up and evaluated the man seated before him in a grey, upholstered chair. Stanley was easily six feet tall. His gray-flannel suit, with French stitching showed a frayed lapel and a torn pocket corner. His jacket showed a hint of red-satin lining that must have been hand sewn inside the jacket. The whole suit was obviously made for a shorter man. Beneath the two-inch hems of his trousers, woolen argyle socks sagged into his scuffed, brown leather brogue shoes. His threadbare black shoelaces were tied with double knots on both shoes. Stan's yellow, cotton shirt with a frayed collar, had buttons missing and was wrinkled like an old roadmap.

Stan scratched his head with nail-bitten fingers, red and raw from his habit. His frizzy, blond hair needed styling by someone competent. Jay wondered if the man ever took the time to go to a barber.

Reworked

Jay scanned the application. Stanley Fisher, born April 9, 1984. He looked up and evaluated the man. Stanley was easily six feet tall. His gray-flannel suit was obviously made for a shorter man and showed signs of wear. Beneath the hems of his trousers, argyle socks sagged into his scuffed, brogue shoes. His yellow shirt with a frayed collar, had buttons missing and was as wrinkled as an old roadmap.

Stan scratched his head with red and raw nail-bitten fingers. His frizzy, blond hair needed styling. Jay wondered if the man ever went to a barber.

Exercise

Rewrite the corrected version of the above example in an alternative setting. The example is a job interview. Use a different scenario.

Good Character Description

Treasure Island, Robert Louis Stevenson, 1883

POV: First person

Genre: Historical Fiction/Adventure

I remember him as if it were yesterday, as he came plodding to the inn door, his sea-chest following behind him in a hand-barrow—a tall, strong, heavy,

nut-brown man, his tarry pigtail falling over the
shoulder of his soiled blue coat, his hands ragged and
scarred, with black, broken nails, and the sabre cut
across one cheek, a dirty, livid white. I remember him
looking round the cover and whistling to himself as
he did so, and then breaking out in that old sea-song
that he sang so often afterwards: "Fifteen men on a
dead man's chest...."

Exercise

Rewrite the above excerpt from *Treasure Island* so that the
description becomes cumbersome and overblown.

Excerpt, Excellent Description

From an upcoming (as of 2018) novel by Judith McAllister.

Scene: a nearly deserted town in a dystopian future. Miss
Sophie is just meeting another main character, Gabriel.

[Miss Sophie] took the frozen moment to give him
a closer once-over. Though duskier than the Injuns
who had died out at Tall Tree Camp, his overall
countenance seemed pleasing. He was young, she
saw. Perhaps nineteen or so. He stood tall. Smart
peered out through his eyes and she found no sign of
bitterness or cruelty in the set of his full mouth. . . .

Characters in Scenes

Integrating characters seamlessly into a scene helps bring the
story to life. You need to write just enough description to give
a thorough picture without becoming ponderous and overly
detailed.

This is especially true when writing about technical or clinical
scenes and props. Do we need to know that Superman's cape has
French-stitched seams or who made his boots? No. It's enough

that he has a smokin' hot bullet-proof outfit that shows off his muscles of steel.

Put in enough clinical and technical explanation to make the reader comfortable with what you're saying. We don't want to know every little aspect of the flux capacitor (Film: *Back to the Future).*

The exception is in highly technical Sci Fi and some Military or Spy-Thriller genres that seem to require Techno-Babble. If this kind of writing is your "nectar of the gods," great. You are in an elite group of talented souls. If not, I suggest not even trying to fake it. There is an art to writing highly technical fiction that most mere mortals cannot fathom.

When to use Techno-Babble

A new gravity dampener has formed around the sub-capacitor which caused temporal fluctuations near the auxiliary gravity core and extended the time-matter field quantum zone.

"I canna' give 'er more, Captain. She's gonna blow!" (Apologies to Scotty.)

In Tech Sci Fi and some Military or Spy-Thriller genres, readers expect to be told about all the bits and bytes of the metatronic warp system or the specs of every nut and bolt in the latest weapons.

When scene-building in other genres, leave out the name of the architect, the designer of the left-handed turnip twaddler, or the composition of the concrete that went into pouring the cornerstone where the mob dumped their latest victim. Also, unless it's important to the story, be careful not to wander into detailed history or back-story about how the scene came to be.

Sci Fi Character and Place Description

Example Excerpt

The Gods Arkhon, Book One, The Prophecy, Anita Burns

Flashy signs and calls from gaudy-costumed sex brokers mixed with the whine and drone of traffic in the travel lanes above.

A pale, thin man reached out to Éndomi as he passed the Juicy Both Ways Club. "You look like a man who could use some company, sir. How 'bout an Ostrovian princess to keep your loins warm tonight?"

"No." Éndomi shoved his fists in his pockets and crossed the promenade to the other side. Cold, with an aching head, he pushed open the doors to the Lucky Pop Café. As he slid into a booth in the far corner, the worn, red faux-leather crackled under his weight. He slumped back and sighed. *Quiet. Good.*

"What'll it be, McKinna?"

Éndomi looked up at the waitress. Telltale signs of age lined her face. *I'd bet there's a sad story behind that smile.*

She shifted from one foot to the other. "Do ya know how to work the menu?"

"Uh, sure. Sorry. Just some kafree and a bagulet, or something."

"We got bagulets. Strawport or citruella?"

He didn't care. "Strawport will be fine. Thanks." He faked a smile. The clink of a chit being deposited into the ancient-looking Musicabox echoed throughout the café. An old tune he recognized from childhood filled the room.

She nodded and walked away.

What am I doing on Radigon? This isn't even an A.I. planet. What a mess. Guilt, self-hatred, and shame flooded him. He ached from it. *I've lost everything. If I go back to Arkhon, or return home, they'll know what I've done.... Urias surely knows. Has she told everyone? Are they hunting for me?* A groan escaped his throat. *I'll be sent to the island.*

The waitress placed a chipped cup on the table and a carafe of hot kafree. "Bagulet is heatin'. Be a sec." She walked away.

He noticed her slight limp. His painful thoughts faded as he wondered about her. *I'm guessing she was beautiful, once.*

.13.

Showing is Better than Telling

The phrase "Show, don't tell" is almost a cliché, but it's one of the most important edicts of writing fiction.

Many of the manuscripts I edit contain too much "tell" and too little "show." Why? Maybe because it's easier to just say what happened rather than struggle to find the words that really paint a picture and bring the reader into the scene, action, or the character's head.

As much as possible, let the readers feel, see, taste, touch, and hear what's going on as if they were there. Telling through a list of he said she-said and he did she did, is snore-inducing. Bring it to life.

There's a reason why many of us fell asleep in high-school history classes but were riveted by the same story when we watched it as a movie, or read it as a novel. A movie or well-written book brought us into the lives of the characters. It had drama, emotion, danger, triumph. History class was pretty much a litany of dates, names, and events.

But be careful of overdoing. Remember each word, sentence, paragraph, and scene has to be relevant to the story. Human minds are messy and jump around in chaotic ways. Don't let that spill out on your pages.

Telling

POV: Third person.

Thomas is thinking about his future as a missionary.

> As Thomas leaned over the railing of the SS Raj, his stomach tightened at the thought of what lay ahead—a new life in a strange land.
>
> He looked at the Bible he carried everywhere with him and prayed to be an instrument of God in his work in this wild and forsaken land. He thought about what he knew of the large Hukawng Valley jungles bordering Assam. Originally it was called Jukaung by the Kachin people who lived there. It means "cremation mounds," because the Kachin had, at one time, expelled or enslaved the other ethnic peoples—
>
> Shan, Chin, and Palaung.
>
> Until the iron fist of British rule in 1401, the people of the Patkai Mountain range to the west were constantly at war....

Sounds like a history book. It's "telling" and full of fact-stuffing (see Chapter 15 Fact-stuffing). Most of that information would be more interesting if it were woven into the story through action, dialogue, and internal thought.

Showing

> Thomas leaned over the railing of the SS Raj, his stomach tightened. *I'm about to start a new life in a strange and exotic land.* He remembered what he'd read about the Hukawng Valley jungles. It was a violent place for centuries. *It's good that people of God are coming to bring the word of Peace to these people.*
>
> That thought comforted him, but only a little. Tales

of cannibalism and unspeakable horrors infiltrated his mind. He gripped his Bible and prayed. "Lord make me an instrument of thy love. Let my hands do thy work." Warmth spread through him and he knew that his prayers would be answered.

Telling

POV: third person.

> Jessica was in her grandfather's study. She walked to the bookcase. Her gaze studied the titles. The books were old and leather-bound. She took in a deep breath.

Showing and Expanded

> Jessica ran her fingers over the polished mahogany table in her grandparents' library. She felt at home in this room that hearkened back to a more elegant time.
>
> "Well, what will I read today?" Stepping to the largest case in the room, her gaze swept over the tooled-leather volumes that smelled of dust and age. *Hmmm. Dickens? Shakespeare?* She touched the spines with her fingertips, searching for something that would make her heart leap. "Ah! Robert Service. Yes! *The Cremation of Sam McGee*."
>
> Pulling the large volume from the shelf, she snuggled into the red-leather, wing-backed chair and mused that the seat cushion sagged from decades of gentlemen and ladies spending their afternoons pouring over good reads.
>
> Carefully opening to a random page, her heart skipped a beat as she read the exquisite words,
>
> "There are strange things done in the midnight sun by the men who moil for gold...."

It often takes more words to show than to tell but what a difference it makes in the reader's experience.

More Showing vs. Telling Examples

Telling

Sylvia looked like she was going to cry.

Showing

Sylvia's squint and trembling lips set off alarms in my head.

Telling

Randall might puke any minute.

Showing

"Uh-oh." The green tinge on Randall's face along with his glassy eyed-stare and the white patches around his mouth warned Jeff that his friend was about to hurl chunks of Margarita Fajita Burrito.

Telling

Brenda listened to Anna whine and bitch.

Showing

Brenda tried to focus on something other than the whiny, bitchy voice of her so-called friend, Anna. It was like listening to a dentist's drill. All she wanted to do was escape to somewhere —anywhere—else.

When is Telling is Okay?

Because you can't, or shouldn't, give a description of every step, thought or action that the characters do or have, sometimes you must "tell." If you can't just skip over some details with a scene break, you might have to just say, "he did…" The trick is to know when it's necessary and when it can be avoided.

Although describing action is necessary, it would be horribly ponderous, for example, to write all the thought processes and movements involved in reaching out to shake someone's hand.

Example

Note: The following is ludicrous and I hope you would never write this much unnecessary detail.

> I looked at his hand and detected movement. His fingers straightened and he began to raise his right arm toward me.
>
> This told me that he was expecting a handshake. I took in a breath, smiled, and extended my arm out toward him. He grasped my hand first and tightened his fingers around mine. I followed suit. He led a pumping action for a second or two then released my hand and returned his arm to a relaxed position at his side. I did the same.

Perhaps, a simple "I shook his hand" would have sufficed.

Whenever possible, the words you use to describe an action from major characters should convey the emotion or intent behind that action. For example, the word "walk" doesn't say anything about what the character is thinking or feeling. Words such as: strode, stomped, lumbered, swaggered, or shuffled convey something of the internal process of the walker.

You can also use descriptions such as: walked with a hitch, with a jaunty walk, or shuffled with a stiff gait. Sometimes, though, just saying "walk" is appropriate. We don't always have an internal process that affects how we move from one place to another.

Showing Intent Through Action

> Michael gently placed his hand on Charlie's shoulder. "Tell her straight out. Do you really think she doesn't already know? I'm sure she has an agreement with someone on the Board to tell her the minute your resignation came through."

In the above example, Michael "put his hand on Charlie's shoulder"—an action. It's telling, but is meant convey an emotion of compassion and understanding. If he had "gripped" the shoulder, it would have conveyed a different emotion.

Showing intent through action, 2

Mark held the car door open for Sheila. He tried not to stare at her long, shapely legs as she slid onto the dark, leather seat.

In the second example, Mark held the car door open for Sheila—an action. It's telling. But the sentence also holds a glimpse into how Mark is feeling and what he might be thinking. How Mark held the door open is unimportant.

If Mark had been feeling stronger emotion such as anger, irritation, or impatience, he could have "gripped the car door handle," or "jerked open the door," but in the example, he's focused on her legs.

More Examples of Telling and Showing

Telling

Mary couldn't sleep. The night didn't cool off as it usually did and the morning sun shining through the window promised another hot, muggy day. With the air conditioner broken, her nightgown stuck to her sweaty skin.

Showing

Mary sat up in bed, and tugged at the nightgown that clung to her damp skin. "Shit. When is this heatwave going to break? Better yet, when will the air conditioning be fixed?" She glanced at the thermometer on the wall by the window. "Geez. It's dawn and already hot enough to cook a lobster. I think I'll go and stick my head in the freezer."

Telling

The thinner man was the sports car mechanic, complete with calloused hands and greasy, black-lined fingernails.

Showing

As I sized up the two men in front of me, I reckoned the tall, lanky one was the mechanic. His black-lined fingernails and calloused hands were a dead give-away. "Hi, I'm Stan. I hear you're the best sports car specialist in town."

Telling is like informing. It often accompanies Passive Voice (see Chapter 5. Verb Tense). Passive voice often leads to telling.

Author Intrusion

Author intrusion is the writer projecting him/herself into the story. It is an "aside" or a "by-the-way" statement, a declaration, or explanation that is unnecessary for the story to move forward.

This is a distracting interruption that upsets the flow. Sometimes it's when one of the characters starts pontificating or lecturing in a way that creates almost a detour from the story.

Before the 20th century, it was common for writers to intrude with a comment about the scene or something that was hidden from the characters. Authors would step away from the story and speak directly to the reader.

This comes from a theater tradition called, "The Fourth Wall." An actor would periodically step to stage-front and speak directly to the audience.

A classic example of author intrusion comes from the 1845 novel, *The Count of Monte Christo*, by Alexander Dumas. At the beginning of chapter two, Dumas writes, "We will leave Danglars struggling with the demon of hatred, and endeavoring to insinuate in the ear of the shipowner…." It is several paragraphs before Dumas brings the scene back into the story

with "…a well-known voice behind him exclaimed, "Father —
dear father!""

Author intrusion can successfully be used as a literary device.

Example Excerpt

The Princess Bride, William Goldman.

Goldman intentionally wrote this book with author intrusion
in mind.

> The year Buttercup turned ten, the most beautiful
> woman lived in Bengal, the daughter of a successful
> tea merchant. This girl's name was Aluthra, and her
> skin was of a dusky perfection unseen in India for
> eighty years. (There have only been eleven perfect
> complexions in all of India since accurate accounting
> began.) Aluthra was nineteen the year the pox plague
> hit Bengal. The girl survived, even if her skin did not.

In the Classic novel, *Jane Eyre*, author intrusion is frequent.
One example is at the start of Chapter Eleven: Bronte speaks
directly to the reader.

> A new chapter in a novel is something like a new
> scene in a play; and when I draw up the curtain
> this time, reader, you must fancy you see a room in
> the George Inn at Millcote, with such large figured
> papering on the walls as inns have; such a carpet,
> such furniture, such ornaments on the mantle-
> piece….

However, since the subtitle of this book is, *An Autobiography,*
perhaps it's appropriate for her to speak directly to the reader.

In film, you can see author intrusion in many successful
comedies, including *Ferris Bueller's Day Off.* All through the film,
Ferris talks to the camera as if speaking directly to the audience.
At the end, he is shown coming out of the shower in a robe. He
looks into the camera and says, "You're still here? It's over!"

In contemporary writing, author intrusion is often unintentional
and more subtle than in the late Eighteenth and early Twentieth

centuries. The writer might be describing a scene from one character's point of view then insert an opinion of their own.

Example

Louise inhaled the fresh, crisp air. This is just what she needed—to get away from the city.

The multi-colored flowers covering the field in front her beckoned as their sweet fragrance wafted to her on the breeze. She didn't even notice the beehive in the tree behind her.

Did you spot the author intrusion above? "She didn't even notice the beehive in the tree behind her." If she didn't notice it, she wouldn't know about it. Only the author would know about the beehive.

Exercise

Rewrite the example to include the beehive so it isn't an author intrusion.

Don't Interpret for the Reader and Don't Explain

When you're immersed in a story, you don't want the author explaining everything. You want the words to show what the character is feeling or doing. If you explain, you venture into intrusion territory—when the author is a narrator and telling the reader what the text means.

Explaining and Telling 1

Joseph had been wronged by someone he'd trusted with his money. He shouted at Sig that the man who cheated him wouldn't get away with it. He pounded his fist on the table. "I won't stand for it. He will pay for what he did to me." Joseph was angry.

Reworked

Joseph felt his face flush with heat. His heart pounded and his breath came quick and deep. "How could the courts let that man get away with this!" He pounded his fist on the table and scowled at Sig. "I won't stand for it. He will pay!"

"Relax," said Sig, steepling his fingers. "You have a good case. We can win this."

Joseph clenched his teeth and pointed his finger at Sig. "I won't let you slack off on this one. Stay away from the horse track and focus on my case or I'll hire someone else!"

Explaining and Telling 2

"Stop sniveling. It's a weakness." Jack didn't like people who gave into to emotions—even his only son. Emotions weren't manly. He was a man's man and wasn't going to let feelings turn his boy into a sissy.

Reworked

"Stop sniveling. It's a weakness." Jack snatched a handful of tissues and threw them at the boy. "Suck it up and be a man. Men don't cry. Do you want to turn

_.15._

Fact-Stuffing

If you think your readers need to know certain facts in order to understand the story, find a way that doesn't create a list, or a lecture. A character giving another character a lot of factual information, or the author telling us a load of facts interrupts the flow of the story and annoys the reader—especially if it's in the "as you know, Jeffrey...." format.

"As you know" Fact-Stuffing

> Sheldon stabbed a finger at the map on the table. "Jeffrey, as a geologist, you know we will be trekking across the Mojave Desert. This region has oscillated in climate many times in the past. When man first arrived in the Mojave, at the end of the Pleistocene era, some 10,000 years ago, it was not the same as we see it today. It was much cooler and wetter, with lakes, streams, and marshes. It had plentiful vegetation and animal life."

If you need to fit in facts about something in your book, find a way to weave it into the scene without having a character tell someone about it with the "as you know" method.

"As you know" fact-stuffing, 2

> Sally placed her mug on the table and stared at her sister. "As you know Anna, I was adopted by our parents but they raised me as their real daughter. When they died, they left us equal shares in the estate."

If the sister doesn't know how they grew up, she's lived under a barrel most of her life.

In the age of social media, online book reviews, and such, the word gets out fairly quickly that a book is badly written. Keep your writing clean lean and clean and don't regale the reader with facts that add little or nothing to the story, do not advance the plot, nor reveal anything important about the characters' motives or personality.

In the pre-TV and movie era, writers were often expected to paint detailed pictures of the environment and to speak directly to the readers. This author intrusion was a vehicle for fact-stuffing. Lines such as, "And now, dear reader, I must interrupt our little tale to tell you that...." were common. (See chapter 14, Author Intrusion)

Author Intrusion and Fact-Stuffing

The Three Musketeers, by Alexander Dumas

POV: Third Person Omniscient

Genre: Historical Fiction/Adventure

> On the first Monday of the month of April, 1625, the market town of Meung, in which the author of ROMANCE OF THE ROSE was born, appeared to be in as perfect a state of revolution as if the Huguenots had just made a second La Rochelle of it. Many citizens, seeing the women flying toward the High Street, leaving their children crying at the open doors,

hastened to don the cuirass, and supporting their somewhat uncertain courage with a musket or a partisan, directed their steps toward the hostelry of the Jolly Miller, before which was gathered, increasing every minute, a compact group, vociferous and full of curiosity.

In those times panics were common, and few days passed without some city or other registering in its archives an event of this kind. There were nobles, who made war against each other; there was the king, who made war against the cardinal; there was Spain, which made war against the king. Then, in addition to these concealed or public, secret or open wars, there were robbers, mendicants, Huguenots, wolves, and scoundrels, who made war upon everybody. The citizens always took up arms readily against thieves, wolves or scoundrels, often....

This information may be important to the overall setting of the story but should be woven into the action and the scenes instead of the author telling the reader.

Classic novels are often difficult for modern readers to enjoy. Their formal language, lengthy descriptions, author intrusions, and fact-stuffing are too ponderous for a world accustomed to sound bites, the visual media of television and movies, and the Internet with its short, to-the-point text.

Readers want authors to cut out the fluff and get to the "meat" of the story.

Exercise

Rewrite the scene from *The Three Musketeers* to be less of a fact-stuffing lecture and more of scene that involves action, character, dialogue, and internal thought. Use modern language.

How to Avoid Author Intrusion and Fact-Stuffing.

Although it's important for you to know your characters inside and out, by now it's probably clear that it's a mistake to dump that information onto the reader all at once. It's also important to research your facts, history, technology, and such, but don't put all that into your book. If, for example, the character is driving a 1934 Buick, you don't have to write about the history of the car company.

- Use dialogue and question and answer to include some facts that are important to the story.

- Have the character go over some facts in his/her mind to piece together the clues to the mystery, but don't drag them out.

- Remember to show reactions to the information; otherwise, it's just a report.

- Have the character discover things a little at a time instead of all at once.

- Use an interview to bring out some facts.

- Have your character give a speech. Keep it brief.

- Have some facts come out in the news or on the Internet or TV.

- Use flashbacks but remember to be brief and make sure they include an emotional hook.

.16.

Language & Grammar

"I say, Neville, properly spoken English is that to which I have become accustomed."

Before Mark Twain, casual language in fiction was uncommon. It's not that people really talked with stilted, grammatically precise language in daily life; it's that literature was expected to be written in proper English (or any language.). It was a sign of education and refinement.

Unless it's in character-appropriate dialogue or internal thought, it's a bad practice to violate too many grammar or punctuation rules. Keep it casual but still grammatically (mostly) correct.

If, however, your characters are meant to speak in a particular jargon or style, write their dialogue and internal thought using the language, syntax, and grammar the way they would. For instance, an inner city gang member would probably not talk like a university professor or a scientist.

Inappropriate Language for the Character

I looked over the grease-stained menu in the only diner open at 4 a.m. The neon sign in the window flashed Charley's Place. Hot Coffee. Cold Beer.

"Have you made your selection, sir?" The frowsy, middle-aged waitress raised an eyebrow and stared at me through thick mascara and bright-blue eye shadow. Her roughened hand gripped the tablet, showing scarlet nail polish that had seen better days.

"I'll have the number eleven. No tomatoes."

"Perfect choice." She snapped her chewing gum as she scribbled my order on her pad then tucked the pencil behind her ear. "It will only be a few minutes." She turned and shouted toward the kitchen, "The gentleman will have the number eleven. He prefers no tomatoes."

Reworked

"Whad'll ya have, handsome?" The frowsy, middle-aged waitress raised an eyebrow and stared at me through thick mascara and bright-blue eye shadow. Her roughened hand gripped the tablet, showing scarlet nail polish that had seen better days.

"I'll have the number eleven. No tomatoes."

"Gotcha." She snapped her chewing gum as she scribbled my order on her pad then tucked the pencil behind her ear. "Be up in a jif." She turned and shouted toward the kitchen, "Number eleven. Hold the red!"

Do you see how the corrected version of this scene makes the waitress more real and believable?

Exercise

Write a scene where two people of different social or ethnic backgrounds have a short dialogue. Make their language match how you describe them.

17.

Narration

Narration is when a character or an unknown omniscient being is telling the story or talking to the reader. Some narration is needed in Third Person POV. It even helps the flow of the text. It's required in academic papers or essays and non-fiction. In fiction, however, too much of it can get in the way of enjoyable reading and become author intrusion (see Chapter 14, Author Intrusion).

A good example of narration handled well is Frank Herbert's *Dune*. The story is told in flashback as if the narrator was telling a story from long ago.

Excerpt Example

Dune, Frank Herbert, 1984

Names and pictures, names and pictures from man's Terranic past—and many to be found now nowhere else in the universe except here on Arrakis.

So many new things to learn about—the spice.

And the sandworms.

A door closed in the other room. Paul heard his mother's footsteps retreating down the hall. Dr Yueh, he knew, would find something to read and remain in the other room.

Now was the moment to go exploring.

Paul slipped out of the bed, headed for the bookcase door that opened into the closet. He stopped at a sound behind him, turned. The carved headboard of the bed was folding down onto the spot where he had been sleeping. Paul froze, and immobility saved his life.

Note that beginning with "A door closed," the story switches to Third Person, Paul's POV. Before that the narrator told the story.

Narration is difficult to do well. The reader will become quickly bored if it's too long or becomes intrusive.

Compare the above excerpt from *Dune*, to the one below from the 19th century classic, *A Tale of Two Cities*, Charles Dickens.

Although he was no Mark Twain, Dickens' style is a bit more casual than the norm for that period. Today, however, this style would be considered tedious and nearly incomprehensible by many readers.

Example Excerpt

A Tale of Two Cities, Charles Dickens, 1859

It was the best of times, it was the worst of times, it was the age of wisdom, it was the age of foolishness, it was the epoch of belief, it was the epoch of incredulity, it was the season of Light, it was the season of Darkness, it was the spring of hope, it was the winter of despair, we had everything before us, we had nothing before us, we were all going direct to Heaven, we were all going direct the other way—in short, the period was so far like the present period, that some of its noisiest authorities insisted on its being received, for good or for evil, in the superlative degree of comparison only.

There were a king with a large jaw and a queen with
a plain face, on the throne of England; there were a
king with a large jaw and a queen with a fair face, on
the throne of France. In both countries it was clearer
than crystal to the lords of the State preserves of
loaves and fishes, that things in general were settled
for ever...

Exercise

Rewrite Dickens' opening paragraphs in a more modern style.

.18.

Actions and Reactions

Correct Order is important.

You wouldn't have someone yelping before they stubbed their toe, but often writers describe actions and reactions out of logical sequence or have characters reacting too late in the scene.

If you stub your toe, you might yell, "OUCH." You do this after the stubbing incident, not before. When writing fiction, it's usually a good idea to write the action first then the reaction. Show the cause, then the effect. If that's not done, the reader has a momentary brain-fade and has to go back and read again to figure out what you intended to say.

Action and Reaction Out of Order

> "Surprise!" The crowd popped up from behind the furniture.

This indicates that the crowd yelled, "Surprise" before they popped up from behind the furniture. It would be better to show what happened in the correct sequence and have the crowd pop up from behind the furniture shouting, "Surprise!"

Reactions need to come right after the action or they can be confusing or lose their punch.

In life people sometimes have an internal reaction or emotion in response to something happening in their outer world. If this fits your scene, make sure the reaction or emotion follows the event.

There can also be emotions that lead to an action. In this case, write the emotion, then describe or show the action.

On the other hand, there can be anticipation of an action that could cause a chain of action-reaction-action-reaction.

Action/Reaction Chain.

The hair on the back of Dave's neck stood up as he carefully stepped through the creaky old house. His flashlight illuminated spider webs in every corner. I hate spiders. He shivered and his throat went dry at the thought of them crawling over his body, down his collar or creeping up his pant legs to—

"Aagh!" He jumped back. Something sticky coated his face. His flashlight clattered to the floor as he jumped up and down, sputtering and screeching swear-words while tearing the spider web away. Afterward, he was sure something crawled through his hair then down his neck and onto his chest.

"Shit!" He ran out of the house, tore off the shirt and tossed it into the bushes. Not caring if his boss reprimanded him or even took his badge and gun, he vowed that he wasn't going back in there.

My apologies to arachnophobes reading the above.

Time sequence is also crucial. If you skip around in time, the reader doesn't know what caused which effect.

Examples
Before

Sweat beaded Jane's brow. She entered the sauna.

After

> Jane opened the door to the sauna and stepped in. Almost immediately, sweat beaded her brow.

Before

> Sue screamed after she had distractedly grabbed the hot pan handle.

After

> Distracted, Sue grabbed the hot pan handle. "Ow!"

Before

> Ron strolled through the mall and parked his car in the handicap spot.

After

> Ron parked his car in the handicap spot then strolled through the mall.

Before

> Vince leapt out of the boat and they pulled up to the dock and ran along the pier.

After

> Vince pulled up to the dock, leapt out of the boat and ran along the pier.

Exercise

Write a scene showing a series of actions and reactions in the wrong order then correct it.

.19.

Don't Tell After You Show and Don't Explain.

Don't interpret for the reader. It's unnecessary to explain what just happened. It's like explaining a joke—annoying and it spoils the joke.

Example 1

> All she could do was lay around the house. For days, the only company Joannie had was a gallon of Chunky Monkey ice cream and a bag of potato chips to scoop it. He'd left her and she didn't know if she wanted to go on. She was in emotional pain.

Do we really need to be told that she's in emotional pain? Duh!

Example 2

> Susan fell into the chair, laughing and panting from her dance. The Bluetooth Mp3 player belted out swing music that spoke to her soul. When the song ended, she reached over, picked up her glass and knocked back her fourth shot of Jack.
>
> The next song started.

"Oh, man! I love's me some Glenn Miller." She stumbled to her feet for a solo Lindy Hop but the room spun around her like water down a bathtub drain. "I guess this wasn't a good idea." She flopped back down onto the chair and kept time with her feet. Susan was drunk.

Do you see that the last sentence should be deleted?

20.

Dive in—Deep Point of View

Use internal thought balanced with action and/or external dialogue to put the reader inside your character's head. Show us his/her hopes, fears, confusions, joy, angst.

Internal Dialogue and Actions

Margo, Molly Dillon

POV: Third Person Multiple

Genre: Mystery/Women's Fiction

The small blue shirt fell from Margo's shaking hands and back into the cedar chest. Reaching in to retrieve it, her fingers touched a piece of paper—a piece of paper which caused her hands to tremble even harder.

Mindlessly, she carried the two items into the living room where they slipped out of her hands and down onto the coffee table. As heartache swallowed her whole, she grabbed her jacket from the back of the couch, slammed out the side kitchen door and through the back gate, fleeing into the full-mooned night.

Her breath quickened as she ran—ran from gnarled hands of grief that reached out, yet again, to strangle her. How many times do I have to go through this pain before it finally goes away? Oh, God, how many?

In *Margo*, Dillon's words reveal a lot of depth about the characters.

Internal Thought with Action and Dialogue

The Gods of Arkhon, Book One, The Prophecy, **Anita Burns**

> Shifting her focus, Kradiora gazed at her reflection in the glass. I look so tired and drawn. She pressed her hand to the window. How cold it feels. *I miss the warmth and lushness of home.*
>
> "Enough!" she chided. "It's time to quit for the night." *It's just that I'm used to getting more sleep.*

These examples take you into the heart and soul of the characters. You experience the world from them as if you were them.

Readers Want to Know

Readers want to know how the character feels, what they see, hear, smell, and taste. Reactions to environment or another person need to be shown. Otherwise it's a script of, "Ronald enters stage left and says...."

In a script, the interpretation and nuance is up to the actor and director to decide and develop. As an author, you are actor, director, writer, and producer. You have to use words to convey what is going on with your characters.

.21.

Emotion & Mood

Humorous? Stoic? Dramatic?
Casual? Formal?

Be sure the emotion in your writing fits the situation. Just as language needs to express a character's nature, ideals, beliefs, social class, and ethnic background, emotional reactions need to be appropriate for the scent.

In a dramatic situation, the reactions of the character(s) would probably be more intense than if they were in a meditation ashram or simply kicking back watching TV.

Reactions Too Stoic or Laid-Back for the Scene

"Tom, help me. I've done a terrible thing."

"What did you do?"

"I hit a car on the freeway and drove away. Someone may have been hurt."

"Really? That is bad. Maybe you should turn yourself in to the authorities."

These two seem overly calm about the issue. The scene

doesn't show the immediacy and intense emotions that would probably go along with a hit-and-run incident. Unless they are two emotionless androids, I'd say it needs a rewrite.

Reworked

"Shit! What was I thinking?" Lisa clutched her cell phone with shaking hands. After three agonizing tries, she finally tapped in the right numbers. Her fingers trembled and tears blurred her vision.

Close to panic, she held her breath as John's phone ring once, twice, three times. "Pick up. Pick up. Please, please. Don't—"

"Hi, Lisa."

"John." She let out a long breath. "I—I don't know what to do." Fear set her teeth chattering. "I'm freaking out h—here." Her mouth turned dry and her heart raced. "I've done something terrible. I'm so scared." A sob caught in her throat. "I don't know what to do. I've never done anything like that. It's—"

"Lisa. Calm down. You're not making any sense. What happened? Tell me. I'm here for you but I need to know."

"Yes.... Yes...." She blew out a breath and raked her fingers through her hair. "I ran into a car on the freeway and—and...Mother of God! What was I thinking? I just left them there." She pounded the heel of her hand to her forehead. "There were children in that car, but I just floored it and took off!"

"Hit and run? You left the scene of an accident? How bad was it? Do you think anyone was hurt?"

She shouted into the phone. "How the hell would I know! I took off!" Sobbing, she pleaded, "Oh, God, don't let there be anyone hurt or dead. I couldn't live with myself."

"I'll be right over. We'll sort this out. Don't do anything or call anyone until I get there."

"I knew I could count on you. Hurry, please."

The rewrite example fits the incident much better. Volatile, roller coaster emotions from helplessness, to anger, to guilt, and back again.

Chewing Scenery

Although intense emotions are correct when called for, melodrama is rarely appropriate—unless you have a character who is a drama queen. Melodrama might be all right on TV "soaps," but in writing, don't use it.

Over-reacting

Sue has had one date with Jay. She sees him in town with another woman, shopping in a bookstore:

Sue clutched at her throat. "Oh, my God! He cheating on me!"

She snatched her cell phone out of her bag and called her best friend. "Beth. OhmyGod, OhmyGod, OhmyGod. What am I going to do? Jay is with another woman! I can't let him see me." She ducked behind a tall display case. Tears streamed down her face. "I thought he was the one! How could he do this to me!"

In that scene, unless you're writing about a psychopath, it's pretty extreme.

Have a sense of how intense or powerful words are. Use them if they fit the situation. Words like, frenzy, bliss, ecstatic, horrific, infuriated are strong. Don't, for example, use terrified if the character is simply worried.

Emotional Shifts

People need time to process. With the exception of Sally Field's character in the film, *Steel Magnolias* , people generally won't jump from one emotion to another without a bridge or a reason. If you're depressed, you won't suddenly feel joy. Give a reason and a process for characters to shift their feelings.

Example: Emotional shifts

Loren stood at the bay window. The gloomy, overcast day fit his sense of futility. *I should have studied more. How could I have failed that exam? Now I have to wait another year to transfer to university.* He shivered when wind rattled the glass pane. The cold, clammy feeling squeezing his insides grew more intense. *Another year without a life of my own. Another year of my mother treating me like a child.*

He absently stared at the open field of wheat across the road. After a moment, the dark clouds parted just enough for a ray of brilliant sunlight to slice through the greyness of the landscape. A patch of bright golden grain shown like a radiant lantern. Some of the heaviness he felt shifted. *Maybe I could go and live with Louise. She understands me.*

The beam of light grew wider and the clouds gradually broke into islands of white on an azure sky. They drifted as if by the breath of some god of the wind. "That's it!" He reached for his phone, hope rising in him as he called his big sister.

This scene couples the weather with Loren's mood, shifting from despair to hope as he watched a storm ending.

Exercise

Write a scene where a character shifts from one dramatic mood to another.

.22.

Conflict

As humans, we thrive on conflict, triumph over adversity, and great odds overcome. Peace and harmony are boring—well, boring to read, anyway. A story without conflict is as tedious as watching Uncle Fred's vacation slides.

We love books filled with suspense where the good guy whips the bad guy's ass but a story needs to have a goal that's worth the main character(s) time and energy to overcome the obstacles.

There has to be something at stake. It could be anything: physical survival, winning a coveted prize, overcoming personal obstacles, reaching for the stars, or solving a puzzle or a crime. Every story doesn't have to have riveting, nail-biting tension, but it does need to speak to the reader at a visceral or emotional level.

Nearly every scene should contain some kind of conflict related to the story's goal. Scenes need to have something—confusion, dilemma, a hard decision, worry, "what-if," a fight, danger, a battle of the fittest, or anything that ups the intensity. If there's no tension—intense or mild—the story stagnates.

Scenes that celebrate triumph or take a break from the major tension should relate in some way to the overall goal of the story. Even if your hero is on a train ride, safe and comfy, thinking he's escaped the bad guys, he needs to have some doubt, or some "what if…?" going on in his mind. In good, fiction there is very little rest for the weary until the goal is reached.

In Joseph Campbell's *The Hero with a Thousand Faces*, Campbell points out that thousands upon thousands of stories share the same theme: the unwitting hero is forced into a new life where he/she transforms, overcomes difficult or impossible situations, rights a wrong, saves the day, or revolutionizes something. He/she battles against the odds for the greater good and is transformed in the process.

Excerpt Example

The Hero with a Thousand Faces, Joseph Campbell, 1949

> The agony of breaking through personal limitations is the agony of spiritual growth. Art, literature, myth and cult, philosophy, and ascetic disciplines are instruments to help the individual past his limiting horizons into spheres of ever-expanding realization. As he crosses threshold after threshold, conquering dragon after dragon, the stature of the divinity that he summons to his highest wish increases until it subsumes the cosmos. Finally, the mind breaks the bounding sphere of the cosmos to a realization transcending all experiences of form — all symbolizations, all divinities: a realization of the ineluctable void.

From the tale of Hercules to *The Last of the Mohicans*, to *Star Wars* to *The Hunger Games* it's the unwilling Hero who drives a compelling story.

Remember, conflict can be subtle or dramatic, internal or external. A character grappling with a moral dilemma can be as compelling as a dragon slayer fighting against incredible odds to save the maiden.

Take a look at your plot and scenes. What's at stake? What are the hard decisions? Is there danger, fear, confusion, false confidence, disgust, anger, or worry? Is there courage of some kind? Are there some "teaching" scenes where the characters learn how to deal with the main goal? Are there minor triumphs that help the hero/heroine reach the goal?

Conflict Themes

There are five basic conflict themes and many other possibilities. Below are some examples from classic novels and films that are still popular today.

Man vs Man or Animal

1. *Moby Dick,* Herman Melville—Captain Ahab risks life and limb to chase down and kill the great white whale.

2. *The Wizard of Oz*—Dorothy bravely travels with her three companions toward the Emerald City in spite the Wicked Witch's efforts to destroy her—and her little dog, too (Could also be Man vs. Supernatural).

3. *The Final Problem,* Arthur Conan Doyle—Sherlock Holmes battles his arch enemy, Moriarty, and nearly loses his own life as he plunges over Reichenbach Falls.

Man vs Nature

1. *Robinson Crusoe,* Daniel Defoe—Shipwrecked Robinson Crusoe uses his wits to survive on a tropical island, battling the environment and hostile intruders.

2. *The Perfect Storm,* Sebastian Junger—Ship's crew fights

a brave battle to survive an deadly storm

3. *The Old Man and the Sea,* Ernest Hemingway—Santiago must bring his big marlin back to shore before the sharks eat it (Could also be man vs animal).

Man vs the World (Society)

1. *Huckleberry Finn,* Mark Twain—Huckleberry Finn fights ingrained bigotry as he travels on the river with runaway slave, Big Jim. They battle society's prejudices, and unscrupulous characters bent on swindling them.

2. *To Kill a Mockingbird,* Harper Lee—Atticus Finch bravely defends a wrongly accused black man. Romeo shuns society and falls in love with Juliette, a member of his family's sworn enemies.

3. *Romeo and Juliet,* William Shakespeare—Romeo shuns society and falls in love with Juliette, a member of his family's sworn enemies.

Man vs Self

1. *A Tale of Two Cities,* Charles Dickens—Self-loathing Sydney Carlton finds redemption by sacrificing his life for the woman he loves.

2. *High Noon,* Carl Foreman, screenwriter—Will Kane facing notorious gun *slingers*, alone, on his wedding day because no one in town would back him up. (Could also be man vs man).

3. *The Great Gatsby,*F. Scott Fitzgerald—In the decadent 1920s, nouveau riche, Jay Gatsby suffers constant conflict with his past and guilt over his obsessive passion for the former debutante, Daisy Buchanon

4. **Man vs Supernatural or Technology**

1. *The Lion, the Witch, and the Wardrobe,* In C.S. Lewis—Three children find themselves in an alternate universe fighting the evil ice queen

   2. *The Picture of Dorian Gray*, Oscar Wilde—An upper class gentleman, Dorian Gray, fears aging. He trades his soul so that a portrait he has commissioned continually changes to reflect his cruel, hedonistic nature while Gray never ages nor shows signs of his inner black heart

   3. *Frankenstein,* Mary Shelley—Victor Frankenstein, is a scientist who obsesses over creating life from death. He succeeds in piecing together a man made from parts of corpses. Horrified at his creation, Dr. Frankenstein must confront the backlash of his actions

   4. *The War of the Worlds*, H.G. Wells—Martians and their machines create a reign of terror, destroying everything and everyone in their path. The story is told by an unnamed narrator who takes us through a gripping story of human bravado in the face of insurmountable odds

Many thanks to *cliffsnotes.com*

Every Scene Doesn't Need a Wow

Remember, every scene needn't have major drama. Sometimes the conflict is mild—a question raised, a decision to make that has consequences, a piece of the puzzle to solve. Some scenes don't need conflict at all. Some scenes need to be peaceful and easy-flowing or celebratory. Our nerves and minds need interlude. But that respite still needs to move the story forward—have a reason for being there.

Pace your drama, conflict, strife, or obstacle so they form a rhythm of tension and quiet. Too much tension loses readers. Long battle scenes can become just so much noise. Too much strife will make us tune out or become inured to it. Too little tension bores readers. Strike a good balance between the two.

.23.

Editing & Grammar

Kill Your Darlings

You've probably heard the phrase, "kill your darlings," or "murder your darlings." It was first coined by Arthur Quiller-Crouch in his 1914 lecture, *On Style*.

> "If you, here, require a practical rule of me, I will present you with this: 'Whenever you feel an impulse to perpetrate a piece of exceptionally fine writing, obey it—whole-heartedly—and delete it before sending your manuscript to press. Murder your darlings."

So, whenever you find yourself holding onto a pet phrase that you know or suspect is over the top, doesn't fit, or simply doesn't need to be there, just highlight and delete. Grieve if you must, but do it.

I have trashed whole scenes and chapters because, although I loved what I wrote, they bogged down the story and did nothing for the plot or scene.

Sometimes it's best to just delete and start over.

To Gerund or not to Gerund?
That is the Asking.

Gerunds are verbs that act like nouns (sort of) and end in "ing." They aren't especially a bad thing to use. In fact, they're sometimes needed for our modern way of speaking and writing.

For example, "Sally's favorite sport is to swim."

To write this without the gerund, you would have to say, "Sally's favorite activity is to go swimming." Sounds odd and awkward. In that sentence, the word, "swimming" is a verb that we have turned into a noun. There are dozens, maybe hundreds—I didn't really count them—of verbs that English speakers have morphed into nouns.

A search on the Internet turns up a wide variety of confusing sites trying to explain gerunds; however a clear explanation plus exercises and more discussion can be found on *gingersoftware. com:* "A gerund is a verb in its "ing" (present participle) form that functions as a noun that names an activity rather than a person or thing. Any action verb can be made into a gerund."

According to *myenglishpages.com:* "Often we use a gerund for an action that happens before or at the same time as the action of the main verb."

Gerunds in Sentences

With gerund

Coding is a marketable skill.

Without gerund

If you learn to code, you will have mastered a marketable skill.

With gerund

I admit that writing pays the bills.

Without gerund
> When I write, I create a product that pays the bills.

With gerund
> Stealing is wrong.

Without gerund
> To steal is wrong.

With gerund
> I enjoy skiing.

Without gerund
> I enjoy myself when I ski.

Can you see that using gerunds is often appropriate and helps with the flow of communication?

The Demon Gerund

A few writing professionals believe that gerunds are the lowly beasts of the earth and should be shunned whenever possible. In researching this mysterious demon, I found dozens of sites acclaiming the gerund as not only acceptable, but preferable to the convoluted and stilted language that would be required to eliminate them.

Some sites espoused the evils of using gerunds at the beginning of a sentence: "Jogging is fun." Others jumped on a soapbox to claim that the use of gerunds is perfectly acceptable.

According to many in favor of the "okayness" of gerunds, they have a place in good writing, even at the beginning of sentences.

It's only when gerunds create a double meaning or an odd image that they become a problem. Without going into deep-dish English grammar and be forced into the maze of participles, infinitives, and such, be sure your use of gerunds is appropriate and doesn't create an unintended meaning to the sentence

Examples

Wrong

> Ann bought her new running shoes strolling through the park.

Were her shoes strolling through the park?

Reworded

> Ann bought her new running shoes while she strolled through the park.

Wrong

> He clicked his pen writing the grocery list.

His pen wrote the grocery list? Really? All by itself?

Reworded

> He clicked his pen then wrote the grocery list.

Be sure the action you are describing makes sense and is physically possible.

Aching to have gerunds running and jumping through your writing? Have some fun.

.24.

Don'ts

Common Mistakes Writers Often Make

Info Dumping and Fact-Stuffing

Stopping the story to explain something or give lengthy information to your readers.

Preaching and Soapboxing

If you feel a need to make others aware of an issue close to your heart, it's all right to include something about it in your story—subtly. Create a character who is passionate about a cause. Allude to it in covert ways, through action, dialogue, and internal thought. Keep it short and fit it naturally into your scene. Readers don't like being preached to and diatribes annoy them.

Pontificating

This is similar to preaching, but more so. Originally a term from the Catholic Church to indicate an address by a bishop or the Pope, it has come to include someone who talks in a dogmatic and pompous manner. To pontificate properly, you need to be a know-it-all with very strong opinions and the urge to share them.

Pontificate comes from the French word pontiff, meaning, Pope, the head of the Roman Catholic Church, but when used as a verb (pronounced pon-TIF-i-kate), it means "to perform the functions of the Pope or other high official in the Church." When used as a noun, pontificate (pronounced pon-TIF-i-kit) refers to the Roman Catholic Church government, also called the papacy.

Was the above "pontification" annoying to read? Even if you liked it, many readers wouldn't. Bottom line: don't pontificate unless you have a pontificating character. Even then keep it short.

If you must include your genius-level knowledge about a subject, do it in small doses and fit it naturally into a scene. Tidbits here and there go a long way. If you want to include more, add special sections at the end of the book—an afterword, glossary, or a section on the history of the area where your story takes place, or links to more information on the Internet.

A Boat-Load of Back-Story

Brief background information about a character, place, or incident is good if it's needed for the reader understand the story or the motivation of a character.

Keep it light, though, and keep it relevant. Better yet, bring out biographies of the characters a gradually, woven into the story.

If you think you must have a detailed history of characters, do so in a special section at the end of the book or put a link to your author website and place the bios there.

Back-story dumped into the text also falls under another category—Telling

Back-Story with and without Telling

With Back-Story and Telling

Leo was a mechanic. His father was a mechanic. He learned how to fix cars from helping his dad on the weekends. When it came time to choose a college, Leo's choice was clear—vocational school. He enrolled in City Trade School, downtown, on Angelino Street. He found the studies easy—almost as if he'd done mechanical work all his life. When he graduated with honors, he was sure that he'd found his vocation.

Now he was on his way to see Maryanne. She had shown some interest in him, but he wasn't sure about her. She'd dated only jocks in high school and Leo never thought of himself as a jock.

Without Back-Story

Leo pulled into Maryanne's driveway. The only thing visible was the backside of her blue mechanic's jumpsuit and sturdy shop boots. "Hey. I got your text. Having trouble?"

She turned and stepped away from her 1987 Ford Thunderbird. "You bet. I can't figure out what that strange whine is. I've checked everything I can think of, but she just keeps whistling the same tune every time I drive her."

"Step aside and let the master take a look." He grinned as he rolled up his sleeves. Bending under the hood, he inhaled the familiar oily smell of the eight-cylinder engine. "Yeah, I worked on these at school. When I was a kid, my dad had a brand, spankin' new one. They don't make 'em like this anymore."

Maryanne wiped her greasy hands on a shop towel. "Any hope, Doc?"

He held his breath as she leaned in close and locked her baby blues onto his.

This scene brings out a lot about the characters without presenting a biography.

.25.

Eyeballs on the Floor and Disembodied Body Parts

Unless you are writing an "undead" novel, don't have body parts doing things that sound as if they have a life of their own.

Examples

- Valorie's hand reached over and unlocked the door.
- John's eyes landed on the stray dog.
- Mike was so angry his eyes shot daggers at Kevin.
- He dropped his head into his hands.
- She pointed her finger at the bird.

Express action without causing readers to laugh or gag.

Reworked

- Valorie reached over and unlocked the door.
- John's gaze landed on the stray dog.
- Mike was so angry, he shot Kevin a steely look of warning.
- How lowered is head into his hands.
- She pointed at the bird.

Exercise

Rewrite the following:

Her fingers picked at the lint on her sweater.

Her dyes danced all over the room.

His feet barely cleared the fence.

.26.

BOP! WHAM! POW!

Action Scenes

What makes an exciting action scene? The obvious answer is lots of *Bop, Wham, Pow*, but it's how that action is described that will make it riveting—or dull. There is an art to writing good action scenes and whole books have been written on just that subject.

In an action scene, it's best to use short sentences, scanty description, and very little, if any, internal dialogue.

Leave the descriptives out unless they're important to the scene. You don't need to include every sound. Unless you're writing a graphic novel, leave out the *Bop, Wham, Pow!*

Action Gone Wrong

Jackson dodged the fist flying toward him. He looked over and spotted the red vase with blue flowers sitting on the mahogany side table. "That'll make a good weapon." Grasping it in his left hand, he tossed the ginger-jar vase over-hand onto the burglar's head.

Action Gone Right

Jackson dodged the punch. He grabbed a heavy vase from the side table and smashed it over the burglar's head.

In Writing Action

- Show as much as possible and tell as little as possible.
- Stay in the POV. It's best not to switch POV within an action scene or a fight.
- Show emotional reactions, thought snippets, and physical reactions.
- Leave out as many details about the environment as possible.
- Use sensory language: visual, auditory, kinesthetic, taste, smell.
- Use strong, direct language. If you're not comfortable with swear words, use !@#$%^ or use euphemisms. A real person in a fight or strong argument probably wouldn't say something like, "Gee, Robert, what the heck to do you think you're doing?"
- Use sentence fragments when they work.
- Describe the action in short sentences and rapid-fire dialogue.
- Keep the fight brief. Fights that go on for pages and pages become tedious.

Example Action Excerpt

The Gods of Arkhon, Book Two, Weokka, Anita Burns

POV: Third Person Multiple

Genre: Science Fiction/Paranormal

Whipping off his helmet, Lakatoma resisted his

mounting rage. He wanted to strangle Ek-Tonis until the little man squealed, but he choked back his anger. "Where's Weokka?"

Ek-Tonis gasped and stepped back, knocking over a table full of glass vials. "How did you find the Surgeon's lift?"

"Where's Weokka?" he repeated, aiming his weapon.

"T—there." Ek-Tonis whined and pointed with a shaky hand. "EKO's men are burning their way through. We *have* to get out of here!"

Lakatoma lowered his weapon. Shoving the quaking Ek-Tonis out of his way, he crossed the room to Weokka. His feeling of relief was overwhelming. "I'm here, Àjonèy. You'll be safe. I promise."

Just as Lakatoma was about to lift her from the operating table, the door burst open and EKO's men poured into the room.

Ek-Tonis grabbed two breathers from the wall and ran for the lift. A disrupter glanced his shoulder and knocked him the floor. Groaning, he began to crawl.

"That's all I need." Lakatoma gritted his teeth and replaced his helmet then shoved the operating table toward the lift. Raising his weapon, he turned and fired in rapid succession. He moved aside to draw the men away from Weokka.

Cold fury engulfed him. "Die, you pieces of rotting *fushak!*"

Time slowed. He aimed his shots with precision. One down, another fatally wounded, two dead. Six more still firing.

"Direct hit to the abductor longus, left leg," said a voice from his helmet sensors.

"I know!" The searing pain told him exactly where he'd been hit.

The attackers were closing in.

He shouted to a frozen and staring Ek-Tonis, "Get Weokka into the lift. Now!"

Another volley of weapon fire lit up the room as he glanced over and saw the operating table empty. *Ek-Tonis must have carried her inside.*

He dashed for the lift, blasting as he went. They didn't come after him. For a second, he was confused. EKO's men had suddenly stopped fighting and turned toward the hallway. Then he heard it. The war cry was undeniable. The Zabinians had breached the building and were coming to rescue Weokka. When they rushed into the room, hand canons ablaze, the fighting clustered near the door.

Lakatoma took advantage of the few seconds he thought it would take before someone fired on him again. He dove into the lift. The door swished shut.

Weokka, still unconscious, lay on the floor, her head on Ek-Tonis' lap.

Kneeling, he touched her cheek then turned his attention to Ek-Tonis. "You hurt?"

Action scenes should get the readers' adrenaline pumping. There should be danger that the hero could lose. Make it hard to win but don't drag it out. Think in short clips of a scene. Use direct, clear language. Hold introspection and analysis until the battle is over.

.27.

This is the VOICE...

If you've ever been around writers or anyone in the business of publishing or editing, you've probably heard the term, "voice." Literary agents, editors, and publishers often say they're looking for a compelling, fresh, and unique voice.

What does all that mean?

Voice is something elusive, almost esoteric. It defies technical definition but is immediately recognizable. It draws us in and keeps us reading.

Although a fresh voice is something editors say they are looking for, they're often hesitant to risk publishing something that doesn't fit the norm. J.K. Rowling is one example. When she tried to get her first Harry Potter book published, it was too far outside the accepted. Short-sighted publishers thought the books too long for middle-grade readers. After numerous rejections, one editor recognized her unique, fresh, and compelling Voice.

It took Rowling years to be published, but look what happened. She is now one of the most successful and widely read authors in the world and the first billionaire writer.

Alex Haley had a similar problem. His amazing book *Roots:*

The Saga of an American Family was not only different, it was controversial. His voice was too unique for most publishers. There's a rumor that he told a reporter he'd wallpapered his office with rejection slips.

His book went on to be published in thirty-seven languages and he won a special Pulitzer Prize for his work in 1977. Roots was adapted into a television miniseries for ABC and broke the record of 130 million viewers.

How Can You Develop a Great Voice?

Each writer must find his/her own Voice. But here are some tips I found helpful in discovering my Voice.

- Don't lecture. If you have a graduate degree or are accustomed to writing academic, legal, or business papers, resist the urge to sound scholarly or "professional." Loosen up. Think of how you talk to yourself or to others at a social gathering. Don't write exactly like that, but find the sweet spot between grammatical and conversational.
- Be clear and as direct as possible. If you find your sentences running on, tighten them up.
- If you give unnecessary explanations, delete them
- If you find yourself writing long words that are not in common use, throw them out.
- Write tight, streamlined sentences that pack a punch or evoke emotion.

Extreme

The infant, reclining in a supine position within
the constructed furniture that the child, by normal

routine, slept within, was positioned within the fork
of a forest plant of the Acer Linnaeus genus.

When minute changes in the atmospheric pressure
vacillated, the ramus of the acer linnaus oscillated. As
excess force was placed upon the ramus, it could no
longer support the poundage and it fractured away
from the acer linnaeus.

As a result, the infant, together with the
constructed furniture, succumbed to gravity and
plunged to earth along with the severed ramus.

Translation

Rock-a-bye-baby, in the tree top. When the wind
blows, the cradle will rock. When the bough breaks,
the cradle will fall, and down will come baby, cradle
and all.

Tips

- Imagine someone reading your words.
- Imagine your ideal readers and write through their eyes.
- Create an imaginary friend and write to him/her.
- For each POV, step into the character's head. Experience the world through his/her body, mind, soul. (See Deep Point of View). Write as if you were the character. George Lucas must have had a lot of fun writing scenes for Darth Vader.
- Always review your story aloud. If you have a computer that will speak your writing back to you, do that, too. Next, read it aloud to a real person. It doesn't seem to matter whether that person is even listening. Something about doing this gives you a completely new perspective. Even with all that, you are probably going to miss a few errors and minor problems—missing quote marks, misplaced comma,

or typos. It's just the way our brains are wired.

- Give each character his/her own personality. A reader should be able to experience each person in your book as unique. Don't make them all sound like clones.

- Be gender appropriate. Writing from the perspective of the opposite gender can be tricky. When I write a scene from a male POV, I always ask at least one man to give me feedback on whether or not the dialogue sounds like a male and whether he would react in the way I'd written.

- The same goes for men writing from a woman's POV. So often women authors feminize their male characters and men masculinize women characters. Sometimes authors make their gender opposites into something they would like them to be in their fantasies. Always have a gender-opposite reader go over your writing.

.28.

Declutter

Like a frat boy living in a room full of old pizza boxes, crumpled chip bags, and crushed soda cans, strewn laundry, and broken appliances, your first draft can bulge with clutter. Empty words abound.

Take a look at your writing and clean it up. Trim away extra words that bog down your sentences.

Rewrite sentences littered with filler words and weak phrases such as:

- it was
- there was
- there were
- of the
- to me
- that
- she (he) saw (heard)

Sometimes the above are needed, but often they can be eliminated to bring more life to your sentences and give them punch.

Examples

Cluttered

There was a firefly that danced around the tree in the light of the moon.

Uncluttered

A firefly danced around the tree in the moonlight.

Cluttered

It was the donuts that were covered in a coating of chocolate frosting and sprinkles of many colors, that were, to me, some of the most tempting delicacies of the day.

Uncluttered

The chocolate-coated donuts covered in sprinkles tempted me the most.

Or, show instead of tell:

I am powerless to resist the temptation of chocolate-coated donuts covered in sprinkles.

A Scene Without Clutter

The character is at a party, looking at the food table.

I stared, glassy-eyed, at a tray laden with Donuts, or "don't-nuts" as my mother always termed them. They beckoned me with an almost supernatural power, drowning out pitiful cries from a plate full of carrots, celery, and sliced peppers. "Turn away from the dark side! Come to us and bask in the light of fresh veggies," they pleaded.

Too late, the siren-call had gripped my senses. I watched, powerless to stop my hand from plucking a shiny, chocolate-covered donut festooned in brightly-colored sprinkles from its family of glazed, maple, and powdered-sugar cousins.

"No!" I cried in breathy desperation, but the don't-nut only strengthened its alluring spell. Alas, I knew I was defeated when the aromas of the evil one's sweet lusciousness filled my senses.

Well, maybe just a nibble, I thought in desperation as I bit into the seductive softness. *Mmm. Have a real bite, said the voice in my head.* I gazed at the damage I had done to the perfect circle of pastry. *Okay, I can't let the rest go to waste.* I opened wide.

Too, soon I awakened from don't-nut trance and found myself staring at the only evidence the temptress left behind—crumbs scattered on my shirt and a few sprinkles stuck to my fingers.

Alas I have once more lost to the Siren's song. I stuffed shame and guilt into the corners of my mind and filled a plate with carrots, celery, and sliced peppers.

Exercise

Give the following a trim and a rewrite.

As Sonia headed down the staircase into the basement, there were toys and some old newspapers strewn and they were standing in her way.

There were cobwebs of the most annoying kind. And at the bottom of the stairs that Sonia was descending, what she found was a door that was closed and she became frightened of the noises that she had heard from behind it. To her, they seemed as if they were like that of the old, scary movies that her brother used to be fascinated with.

That

Filling your sentences with "that" is like landscaping with Lawn Gnomes. Most of the time you're better off without them.

Remove as many instances of "that" as possible in your writing. How? Read your sentences without them. Do they still make sense? If so, throw them out. If not, keep "that" in. You may be surprised at how many times you just inserted "that" without thinking about it.

Exercise

Can the following sentences do fine without "that"?

- She said that she would be here by ten.
- The cat that I rescued is adorable.
- I am that I am. I'm Popeye the sailor man.
- It's just that I'm very sensitive to pollen.
- That's the problem.
- He's supposed to pick up the package that I have waiting for me.

If removing "that" changes the meaning of the sentence or makes it unclear, either reword or leave it in.

Example of a Necessary "That"

Sue remembered that all the ladies in the department needed to bring a potluck dish.

If "that" is taken out of the above sentence, it could mean Sue remembered all the ladies in the department—not that she remembered they needed to bring a potluck dish.

It Hurts Only for a Little While

Decluttering can sometimes be a painful process, whether it's cleaning out your basement or your writing. It's tough but after you're done, you'll have a much more engaging and readable story. Then, maybe treat yourself to a don't-nut.

.29.

Repeated Words and Similar Phrases

For some reason that linguists or psychologists could probably explain, words or phrases repeated within a few paragraphs or even a couple of pages, grate on our nerves or feel somehow wrong. Yet, nearly all writers do this in first drafts—even experienced, best-selling authors. Redundancy sprouts in our prose like weeds in a garden.

A Weedy Garden

> As I approached my front door, I noticed it was open a crack. Cautiously I put my hand on the doorknob and inched the door open. "Hello?" I called inside. Hearing nothing, I swung the door open wider and tiptoed through the doorway. "Hello? Is anyone here?"
>
> After listening for a few seconds—it felt more like an hour—I quietly closed the door and tiptoed down the hallway to the kitchen door.

How many "door" words are in the above? Too many.

A Weeded Garden

> As I approached my apartment, I noticed the door was open a crack. Cautiously, I grasped the knob and pushed until I could see inside. "Hello?" I called out. Hearing nothing, I stepped over the threshold. "Hello? Is anyone here?"
>
> After listening for a few seconds—it felt like an hour—I tiptoed down the hallway and left through the kitchen.

Never Let a Good Phrase or Action go to Waste

Another mistake authors often make is repeating actions or phrases. Look over your text. Do you have a lot of deep breathing, rolling eyes, stopping, sighing, ambling, yawning, or racing hearts? In my first draft of *The Gods of Arkhon*, one of the men in my critique group pointed out that I had a lot of characters who seemed to find flat rocks to sit on.

It's often difficult to spot these repetitions yourself. Using your word processor's "find and replace" function can help you locate them. It's all right to have a repeated word or phrase a few pages apart, but don't overdo it.

Subject-Verb-Object

Too often we get in a rut of beginning sentences and paragraphs with a subject followed by a verb, or by a subject-verb-object. The repetitive cadence of this pattern interrupts the reader's involvement in the story.

Vary them so they don't have the same structure.

Example

Theresa understood that Ralph was naturally impatient but surgery takes time—not something that should be rushed. "Will you sit down?"

Ralph stopped in his tracks. "I know it's going to be hours. I'm afraid she's not going to make it. Pacing the floor, helps me will the time to pass faster." He grinned.

Simon approached Ralph, "Take it easy bro. Everything's cool. You're gonna wear a hole in the floor."

Theresa handed Ralph a cup of coffee. "Sit down. You can't control everything. The procedure will take as long as it needs to."

Reworked

Theresa understood Ralph was naturally impatient but surgery takes time—not something that should be rushed. "Be still—please!"

"I know it's going to be hours," he said. "Pacing helps me will the universe into hurrying."

Approaching Ralph, Simon put a hand on his shoulder, "Take it easy bro. Everything's cool. You're gonna wear a hole in the floor."

Theresa handed Ralph a cup of coffee. "Sit down. You can't control everything. The procedure will take as long as it needs to."

Don't sound like a broken record or a talking parrot. It's a sure way to annoy your readers and drag them out of the story. Add variety and watch out for repeated words and phrases.

30.

He said. She said.

Dialogue Tags

Dialogue tags help readers know who's talking but if you add a tag after every sentence, it becomes tedious.

When the source of dialogue is obvious, leave the tags out. On the other hand, if you eliminate too many, it's easy for readers to lose track of who's saying or doing what.

Too Many Tags.

"I'm goin' to the store. We're outta milk," said Jessi.

"Pick up some chips, too?" asked Otis.

"You payin' for it?" asked Jessi.

"I aint got no money," said Otis.

"Then you ain't getting' no chips," said Jessi.

Do you see how the tags get in the way of flow? We know who's responding; however, in a long list of back and forth dialogue, the reader may get lost. Add an action to break the monotony and add color to your scene.

Reworked

Jessi picked up her handbag and headed for the door. "I'm goin' to the store. We're outta milk."

"Pick up some chips, too?" asked Otis.

"You payin' for it?"

Otis tossed his empty beer can across the room. "I ain't got no money!"

"Then you ain't gettin' no chips." Jessi stomped out r and slammed the door behind her.

Vary your sentences to show who's doing the talking or acting to create a flow that keeps the reader engaged.

Keep it Simple

When you do use tags, keep it simple. Don't vary how you identify the source of the dialogue. Stick mostly with he said, she said, he asked, she asked, or the name of the character and said or asked. Use the dialogue itself and descriptive action to indicate the emotional intent of the dialogue.

People who study such things found that the word, "said" is treated like punctuation, an unconscious recognition of its meaning. If you draw attention to the mechanics of the story by adding descriptive words about how the dialogue was delivered, readers will be torn from immersion in the story.

Example 1

"Sam," Rita squealed, "I need help."

"Rita," he pleaded, "I know you can't do this but—"

"No!" she cried. "I can't!"

Sam shouted, "Stop being such a baby!"

"You're the meanest man on earth," Rita sobbed.

Example 2

> "I think this is the spot," Will remarked.
>
> "No. It's over there," Jane countered.
>
> "Well, we could stop and ask for directions," proposed Lilly.
>
> "Are you kidding? Men don't ask for directions," stated Jane.
>
> "Some men do," retorted Will.
>
> "I'll believe that when I see it," replied Lilly.

Not only are there too many tags and static structure (each tag comes at the end of the sentence) in the above, each one having a descriptive is agonizing to read.

Exercise

Rewrite the above so it flows better.

TIP: Read your dialogue aloud then have someone else read it to you. You might be surprised at how helpful this can be to spot inappropriate tags and static structure.

.31.

Adjectives and Adverbs

Adjectives are words or sets of words that modify (describe) nouns and pronouns. Adverbs describe how, when, where, how often, and how much.

In English, adjectives usually come before the word they describe. For example, "The black cat." We can also say, "The cat is black," but this is less common. In other languages, adjectives often follow the noun. In French, the sequence would be, "Le chat noir," The cat black.

Adjectives and adverbs add depth, color, and "aliveness" to your writing. Without them your scene would be sterile, stilted and difficult to understand.

As in all things, however, they can be over used and create a gawdy, messy scene that resembles Miss Pittypat's parlor (from *Gone with the Wind)* instead of one that enhances the flow.

Too Many Adjectives

My gnarly, old grandmother slowly brushed her
shiny, long, wavy, silvery hair with her antique, ivory-

colored, boar bristled, silvery-handled hairbrush.

Reworked

My grandmother brushed her long, silvery hair with her antique hairbrush.

The other adjectives could be added if they were important to the story. Otherwise, if the color and construction of the brush are not needed, leave them out.

Adjectives Come in a Variety of Favors, Including:

Age—young, old, teenage, childish, mature, infantile, recent, ancient…,

Brightness and Color—light, dark, murky, dim, glaring, radiant, black, red, orange…,

Distance—long, far, near, close, outlying, remote, neighboring, at hand, afar…,

Emotion—happy, sad, excited, frightened, funny, cheery, blissful, lonely, ecstatic…,

Function—swinging, work, cooking, sleeping, walking, folding, collapsing…,

Quantity—few, no, little several, many, all, some, every, one, two, three…,

Opinion—good, bad, better, best, worst, splendid, wonderful, awesome, useful…,

Location—north/east/south/west, polar, lunar, latitude/longitude, Africa, Asia…,

Material—wooden, glass, fabric, glass, ceramic, metal, stone…,

Shape—square, round, long, squat, oval, wavy, squiggly, crooked, winding…,

Size and Weight—big, small, tiny, minuscule, huge,

ginormous, heavy, light…,

Smell—reeking, fragrant, acrid, noxious, pungent, musty, sweet…,

Sound—loud, soft, noisy, quiet, deafening, muffled, whispered, pitchy …,

Brightness and Color—light, dark, shadowy, drab, shining, pale, dull, black…,

Speed—fast, slow, rushing, rapid, swift, hasty, brief, snail's pace, rushing…,

Taste—sour, bitter, sweet, salty, delicious, tasty, savory, luscious, spicy, watery…,

Time—early, morning, late, night, day, first, last, delayed, over-due, evening, dawn…,

Temperature—cold, icy, frigid, frosty, hot, scorching, scalding, burning, fiery…,

Touch—smooth, velvety, hard, rough, grainy, slick, brittle, glossy, scratchy, rough, sticky…,

Exercise

Choose five or more adjectives from the list above and compose a scene using them.

Exercise Example

Teenage, dark, old, wavy, black, white, cracked

Diana studied the photo of her mother. The black and white snapshot showed a teenage girl with dark, wavy hair.

She ran her thumb over the cracked surface of paper then tucked it back into the album.

Adverbs

Adverbs describe an action. They tell how, when, where, how often, and how much. Adverbs are also vital to creating an engaging scene. You could say, "The dog ate." Or, you could describe it more with an adverb, "The dog ate heartily." Which one gives a more interesting image?

Many adverbs end in "ly" but not all of them. If they are describing an action or a verb, they are adverbs.

As with adjectives, they also come in many flavors, including:

Certainty (Probability)—probably, certainly, definitely, likely, doubtless, surely

Degree (Percentage)—almost, nearly, barely, quite, totally, thoroughly, too, very

Manner (How)—beautifully, tenderly, well, quietly, lovingly, greedily, frankly

Place (Where)—here, now, there, nowhere, nearby, up, down, backwards, forwards

Time (Duration and Frequency)—before, after, today, tomorrow, yesterday, recently, later, often, always, never, sometimes, yearly, daily, weekly, rarely, normally

Exercise

Use three or more adverbs in a scene.

Exercise Example

Almost, before, daily
> She almost reached her goal—something she'd never done before. Her daily workout seemed to be making a difference.

Adjective and Adverb Qualifiers

Overuse of qualifiers, such as, often, somewhat, usually, pretty, just, mainly, generally, basically, sort of, almost, and a bit make your sentences like my best friend's coffee—weak and watery. They dilute your message or dialogue, weaken tension, and imagery fades.

Too Many Qualifiers.

> Roberta was a bit disappointed that Kyle didn't quite like her new painting. "I sort of thought you would love it very much."

Notice that the word, "new" is an adjective that appropriately describes the painting.

Reworked.

> Roberta was disappointed that Kyle didn't like her new painting. "I was sure you'd love it."

Exercise

Translate the following to eliminate the qualifiers and other problems that weaken your text.

1. Anna was somewhat miffed at the situation. She was a little worried about the time almost running out.

2. I'm basically at the end of my rope. It could be somewhat of an issue if he doesn't come around.

3. "Where do you think you might be going at this late hour of the night? Nowhere fast, I'm thinking. It's horribly late." Charley nearly cried. He definitely slept terribly and was a little too tired to think much about the unquestionably difficult decisions he would have to make. He was very upset at the turn of events.

Scan your text for qualifiers. You might be surprised at how many you include without thinking about it.

Intensifiers are Like, So Intense

Like qualifiers, intensifiers need monitoring. Words such as very, totally, too, extremely, perfectly, truly, actually, particularly, fabulous, incredible, magnificent, wonderful, awesome, and completely are valid words to use but they need to add to the quality of the story instead of being a convenient, quick way to up the ante of a noun or verb.

The word "very" seems to be the most overused intensifier that tenderfoot writers fall in love with. Fortunately, there are dozens of substitutes for "very."

Examples

> **Very big:** enormous, huge, gigantic, vast, substantial, immense, massive, titanic, spacious, whopping
>
> **Very small:** teeny, tiny, minuscule, pint-sized
>
> **Very clever:** genius, precocious (for a child), brilliant, astute, wise, brainy
>
> **Very bad:** inadequate, inferior, disgusting, dreadful, miserable, atrocious, appalling, deplorable
>
> **Very sure:** certain, positive, confident, definite, surely, unhesitating, unwavering, unshapable, guaranteed
>
> **Very good:** perfect, superior, excellent, superb, sterling, splendid, blue-ribbon, awesome, smashing.
>
> **Very pregnant:** This isn't even possible.

Take advantage of a thesaurus to find alternatives to common intensifiers. Think about how much would be lost if A.A. Milne had titled his book, Winnie the Pooh and the Very Windy Day instead of *Winnie the Pooh and the Blustery Day.*

Verily, I say unto you, extraneous adjectives and adverbs will heavily and surely reign down a plague upon your head.

Words Ending in "Ly"

Words (usually adverbs) ending in "ly" can appropriately describe how, where, when, how often, and why something occurs. The trick is to know when they are needed and when they are just frilly window dressing.

Example

The dog carefully sniffed his master's shoes.

"Carefully" is the adverb. Does it add to the description of the dog's behavior? Would you leave it or change it?

Look at your writing and find adverbs. Examine each one. Do they enhance or weaken your writing? Can a stronger, more direct word be substituted?

More Examples

Unnecessary, 1

He walked loudly through the theater.

Corrected

He stomped through the theater.

Unnecessary. 2

Sudden,y, the air turned icy.

Reworked

Without warning, the air turned icy.

Unnecessary, 3

When he heard the firecrackers, he immediately ran for cover.

Reworked

When he heard the firecrackers he ran for cover.

Sometimes an "ly" adverb is the best word for what you want to say. Develop a sense of when and when not to use them.

.32.

Dangling Participles and Misplaced Modifiers... Unintentional Humor

If you're like many people, you wouldn't recognize a participle—dangling or not—if it bit you on the behind. Without going into yawn-inducing descriptions straight from the *Chicago Manual of Style*, just remember that participles are generally "ing" or "ed" words that modify nouns.

Example

Riding his bicycle, Ted pushed himself to the limit.

When participles are used incorrectly, some amusing impossibilities can be described. Participles dangle when they modify something other than what the writer intended.

Dangling, 1

The thief ran from the policeman holding the loot in his arms.

Reworked

Holding the loot in his arms, the thief ran from the policeman.

Dangling, 2

Flying over the lake, Bob saw the flock of snow geese.

Reworked

Bob saw the flock of snow geese flying over the lake.

Dangling 3

Falling over the cliff, the climber lunged to save the child.

Reworked

When the child fell over the cliff, the climber lunged to save him.

Exercise

Write three sentences that contain dangling participles then correct them.

Misplaced Modifiers

Read your text looking for misplaced modifiers. Did you spot the dangler in that sentence? If a sentence can be misread to mean something other than what you intended, reword it.

Misplace Modifiers

With only one eye, the young woman ogled the body builder.

Does the woman have only one eye or was she looking at him with only one eye?

Anna saw the cutest Siamese kitten on the way to the bus stop.

I hope the kitten had exact change for the bus.

With a grin on her face, Mona served birthday
cake to her son on a paper plate.

That must have been a big plate to hold her son. Or, was he
Tom Thumb.

Exercise

Write three sentences that contain misplaced modifiers then
correct them.

.33.

As Smooth as a Baby's Bottom—Flow

To some, flow is one of those nebulous things about writing that, without knowing how, you just recognize. It's like saying, "I don't know anything about art, but I know what I like."

Usually, if you have all the technical parts of writing correct, your writing will flow but sometimes it remains elusive. We don't fully understand every component that makes our prose either flow or turn into lumpy cream of wheat. It's just something you learn to recognize for yourself.

Awkward

>   As soon as the elevator doors began to open, Sally could see the scene in the office suite she worked. Chaos had happened. Something violent had occurred between the time she had left the building had to return to work.

Flow

>   When the elevator doors opened, Sally's jaw dropped. "What the . . .?" The cup holding her iced

tea slipped from her fingers and splattered onto the floor. She checked the panel. "Fifth floor. I'm in the right place."

Holding the "open" button, she swept her gaze around the room. Chaos. Broken glass, chairs and desks upturned, computers smashed onto the floor, paper strewn everywhere.

What happened? Where is everyone?

What components do you think make the Rework flow better than the Awkward?

Exercise

Rewrite the Awkward example in a different way from what I did. Does your version flow?

Awkward

"You're just stupid and you look funny," I was told by one of my best friends at the end of summer camp. Talk about being the most surprised, ever. I paused and didn't even know what to say. I could sense during the prior evening at dinner that two of my friends were upset with me, and I wasn't even sure why they would be.

Flow

In our cabin, on the last night of Summer Camp, Lisa looked up at me and sneered. "You're just stupid and you look funny." said Lisa.

This was a surprise. I didn't know how to answer.

Come to think of it, at dinner, she and Beth were whispering to each other about something. They stopped when I came to the table.

I turned away so Lisa wouldn't see me close to tears. What did I do?

Exercise

Rewrite the above in a different way. Does it flow?

Awkward

I was searching the auction sites on the Internet looking for information on an unusual lamp that was to be auctioned by our competitor. My shaking fingers kept hitting the wrong keys, like a chicken playing the piano.

A screen unknown to me began unfolding. The letters were unknown to me. I studied anthropology and antiques. At that moment, I recognized what the incongruous letters were staring at me. They resembled hieroglyphs I've seen on ancient buildings. They appeared to contain some unfamiliar nuances. I'm positive the bosses left keys to open this screen by accident. Perhaps it wasn't only a mistake, after all, there is no such thing as a coincidence, or so-called accidents. Somehow this was destined to happen. It's like that theory that says the future is happening all at the same time. Some signal is sent to your brain and there it is.

Flow

Sneaking into my competitor's office after hours, I opened his computer using the stolen password my informant had given me. My trembling fingers tapped the keys like a typing chicken as I searched for information about the priceless lamp they would be auctioning off on Friday. When I hit the Return key by mistake, a file filled the screen with odd letters. "What's this?"

Intrigued, I peered at the odd letters. They seemed somehow familiar. Maybe hieroglyphs? *Hmmm. Not Egyptian, though—.* I froze. A loud noise cane from outside the office, then footsteps. I shut off the computer and waited, hoping I wouldn't lose the contents of my stomach. *What am I doing? I'm not cut out to be a spy.*

Luckily, whoever it was walked right past. When I
heard another door open and shut, I let out a breath
with a *whoosh*. Then, heart pounding, I slipped out
and ran for the exit.

Exercise

Rewrite the above example in a different way. Does it version flow?

Too Much of the Same Rhythm
is a Flow-Breaker

Starting each paragraph with subject/verb or writing too many sentences of the same length causes an interruption in the flow. Remember that an author's goal is to have the reader immerse him/herself in the story and not notice the writing itself.

If you go to a theater to see a play or a movie, after a few minutes you forget about the theater itself and are only paying attention to what's on the stage or screen. If something interrupts that, your mind switches to your environment—other people, noises, smells, temperature, and such. It takes your attention away from what you paid an exorbitant amount of money to enjoy.

It's the same with reading. Too much of the same rhythm jerks us out of the story and into a meta-experience of the pages, the words, the environment. Often it makes us start skimming the pages instead of reading them. The story becomes tedious instead of engrossing.

Too Much

Lisa drove to the store and fought her way through
the crowd to get to the sale table.

> Lisa found the purse she wanted just as a large
> woman dressed stretch in pants and faded tee lunged
> for it.
>
> Lisa grabbed the purse and ran out the door. .

Every line starts with subject/verb. Mix it up a little for better flow. Did you spot the other issue in the above example?

Avoid starting successive paragraphs with "He," "She", "They," etc. It's all right to do this within a paragraph so you aren't repeating the character's name too often. Just be sure it's clear who the pronouns are referring to. Replace the pronouns with the characters' names to breakup the chain and/or add actions or internal thoughts.

Exercise

Rewrite the"Lisa" example for better flow.

Too Many "He"

> He looked in the mirror at his ill-fitting suit. He
> wondered if a tailor could take it in for him. He
> thought about how overweight he must have been
> when he last wore this clothing. He tugged the
> waistband. It pulled out from his body at least five
> inches. He thought how much better he felt to be slim
> and trim.

Reworked

> Jim looked in the mirror at his ill-fitting suit. *I'm
> sure a tailor can take this in.* Turning sideways and
> seeing how trim he looked, Jim remembered how
> overweight he'd been just a year ago. Tugging on the
> waistband, it pulled out from his body at least five
> inches.
>
> He grinned and puffed out his chest. "Wow. It feels
> so much better to be slim and trim."

Don't start more than one sentence in a paragraph with a gerund.

Remember gerunds? They generally end in "ing." Starting multiple sentences with gerunds interrupts the flow like boulders in a stream. Once or twice in a paragraph is usually okay but a string of them, or even two in a row is jarring.

With gerunds

Standing outside her boss' office door, Mary listened carefully. Putting her ear to the door, she heard nothing. Grasping the knob she cracked open the door just enough to peer in. Seeing an empty office, she quickly opened the door wide and stepped inside. Heading for the desk, she began to pry open the locked drawer.

Without gerunds

Mary stood at her boss' office, ear to the door but heard nothing. She turned the knob and pushed to create an opening just enough to peer inside. Good. It's empty. She quickly slipped inside and tiptoed to the desk. I have to find out what's inside that locked drawer. With a letter opener in her hand, she began to pry it open.

And, And, And

Too many sentences with "and" interrupts the flow. It's like listening to a five-year-old describe his day:

"And today I went to the store and bought the candy and juice and the man was really nice and he smiled at me and my mom and said how his son looked a lot like me."

With "And" 1

She was thin as a rail and with long and silky hair and big blue eyes.

Reworked
>She was tall and thin. Her long, silky hair set off her big blue eyes.

With "And" 2
>The street vendor wore a long and tattered scarf and he called out to passersby.

Reworked
>The street vendor wore a long, tattered scarf as he called out to the passersby.

Combine Short Sentences to Create More Flow

When you find yourself faced with a string of short, choppy sentences, combine some of them for better flow.

Choppy
>Allen Jenkins was the month's top salesman. He sat at his desk. He felt proud of his accomplishment.

Reworked

Salesman of the month, Allen Jenkins sat at his desk feeling proud of his accomplishments.

.34.

Run-on Sentences and Comma Splices

If you combine sentences, make sure they aren't run-on or comma splices. Run-on sentences and comma splices are complete sentences linked by a comma or conjunction or both.

They are closely related and often confused with each other.

Run-on

- Tim is a smart boy he really loves math, he likes to spend time in the astronomy lab.
- It was a stormy night the clouds covered the sky.
- I went to the store, I bought new shoes.
- Wherever I go I am always happy, I am happy indoors and out.

Exercise

Rewrite the above to eliminate the run-ons and comma splices.

.35.

Semicolons: Devils or Angels?

Semicolons are a great way to link two closely related sentences but they are rarely used in fiction. This little winking symbol seems to disturb many readers of fiction. Leave them out unless there is no other way to express what you want to say.

Examples of Semicolon Use

> When I'm through with the dusting, and I soon will be, I'll be happy to help you with the painting; and that's a promise I'll keep.

Divide and Simplify for More Flow

> As soon as I'm finished with the dusting—and I'm almost done—I'll help you with the painting. That's a promise I'll keep.

36

Redundant, and it's the Same

Although you want your dialogue and text to sound easy and comfortable, in print, redundancy stands out like a clown nose on a walrus.

When you find words written together that mean the same thing, change them to one word that covers the meaning of what you want to say.

Examples, Redundant

From *dailywritingtips.com*

Absolutely Certain

Actual fact

Added bonus

Add an additional

As for example

At the present time

Final outcome

Fundamental basics

Close proximity

Full and complete stop

Definite decision

End result

Enter in

Few in number

First began

For a number of days

Foreign imports

Forever and ever

Free gift

Honest truth

Invited guests

Paired together

Past history

Plan ahead

Possibly might

Postpone until later

Protest against

Revert back

Repeat again

Same identical

Still remains

Therapeutic treatment

Uniquely different

Unexpected surprise

Unintended mistake

Usual custom

Written down

Exercise

For each example, change the above to one word that conveys

.37.

And so it Ends

Writing is an adventure. Live the journey. Read everything you can on how to make your writing magical, compelling, engrossing, and powerful.

There is so much more that I could include in this short guide and I may add to it or publish a second volume, some day, when the muse beats me over the head.

In the meantime, search out resources, read, read, read. Write, edit, write, edit, and create your masterpiece.

"Begin at the beginning," the King said, very gravely, "and go on till you come to the end: then stop."
—Lewis Caroll, *Alice in Wonderland*.